ROALD AMUNDSEN.

Nome, Alaska.

FIRST CROSSING
OF THE
POLAR SEA
by
ROALD AMUNDSEN
AND
LINCOLN ELLSWORTH

WITH ADDITIONAL CHAPTERS BY OTHER
MEMBERS OF THE EXPEDITION

University Press of the Pacific
Honolulu, Hawaii

First Crossing of the Polar Sea

by
Roald Amundsen and
Lincoln Ellsworth

With Additional Chapters by other members of the expedition

ISBN 0-89875-287-6

Reprinted from the 1928 edition

University Press of the Pacific
Honolulu, Hawaii
http://www.universitypressofthepacific.com

FIRST CROSSING OF THE POLAR SEA

CONTENTS

[vii]

Contents

ILLUSTRATIONS

Illustrations

To
*The men who brought
the "Norge" safe across
the Polar Sea.*

ROALD AMUNDSEN AND
LINCOLN ELLSWORTH

CHAPTER I

At a meeting between Roald Amundsen, Lincoln Ellsworth, and First-Lieutenants in the Royal Norwegian Navy Riiser-Larsen and Leif Dietrichsen, at Svalbard in May 1925, the possibility of a flight from continent to continent, via the North Pole, was thoroughly discussed for the first time. At that time we lay ready with our two Dornier Wal seaplanes to pay our first visit into the vast unknown realms of the ice-king. We understood indeed, as our preparations progressed, that this our first venture was to be considered merely as a reconnoitering expedition for the later intended flight over the Polar Sea. How fresh in our memory is that meeting of ours! It was not a grand place of assembly with gilded furniture and upholstered chairs that we met in. On the contrary, two rickety chairs and two camp-bedsteads were the whole equipment. There was no president there, with bombastic phrases and mace in hand. Four men, quiet and serious, had taken their places on whatever offered, chair or bedstead; and, to the accompaniment of the throbbing of the motors of the two waiting seaplanes, the possibility of the greatest flight ever planned was discussed. The foundation-stone of that which should subsequently be styled "The *Norge's* flight across the Polar Sea" was here laid, without ceremony of any kind and without trumpet-blast or fanfare. It was Riiser-Larsen who drew attention to the Italian airship *N* 1 as being the best fitted for the enterprise.

A few days after the meeting the two machines *N* 24 and *N* 25 headed in over the interminable waste of ice in order to gather experience for the newly planned expedition.

The flight of 1925 is so well known that we shall not go further into this subject. Only we must protest when it is called—as we have so often seen it called in the world's Press—a failure. Our object was to study the conditions over the waste as far as was possible, and this object we fully attained, even with our lives at stake. Our assumption that the atmospheric conditions over the ice-masses of the Polar Sea were specially suited for a dash with airships we found fully confirmed. No disturbances of any kind presented themselves on the long flight to 88° N. and back again. We were also quite convinced that airships at the present time are the superior of all flying-machines. It takes so little to put an aeroplane out of action. A small leakage or a loose screw is enough to compel a forced land-ing, and that, too, is more than risky in a region where no landing-places are to be found. It is different with an airship. If, in this case, a motor gets out of order, one merely stops and repairs it. Fog is the second bitter foe a flying-machine has to reckon with. A forced landing in a fog is certain death.

After our return from this flight we at once sought to get into touch with the then Colonel Umberto Nobile, the constructor and builder of *N* 1. He very readily met us, and, after a short time, presented himself for a conference in Oslo. The first meeting took place in Amundsen's home in Bundefjord, between Amundsen, Nobile, and Riiser-Larsen. According to the particulars we here received from the constructor of the airship we were still further confirmed in our conviction that *N* 1 was the best suited for this long flight. Nobile was able moreover, to announce that the Italian State, to which the airship belonged, would prove very indulgent in the event of the purchase of the ship. Just as in the previous year's flight, we this time also took the Norwegian Aero Club into coöperation, and we especially owe to its president, Dr. Rolf Thommasson—editor and doctor of philosophy—our warm thanks for his zealous endeavors and interest in the undertaking.

Shortly after this Amundsen and Riiser-Larsen went to Rome, in order to sign the contract for the purchase of *N* 1. Thanks to Mussolini's great interest in the matter, it was very easily arranged and on excellent terms. It was decided that N 1, after a number of alterations, should be ready at the beginning of 1926, and that then the Norwegian crew should go to Rome, and there under Nobile's instructions, obtain practice in the maneuvering of the vessel.

Soon after his return from Rome, Amundsen went to the United States, in order, by means of lectures on the flight to 88° N, to raise money for the coming expedition. Later Ellsworth announced that he would, on certain conditions which were accepted, contribute a sum of a hundred thousand dollars in aid of the new enterprise. Upon this generous offer the foundation of our enterprise was laid. As Ellsworth's assistance in these two undertakings has been repeatedly mentioned, and not always quite correctly, it may be of interest to stay for a moment and cast a glance on what these expeditions owe to him. Amundsen himself mentions, in his introduction to the description of the previous year's flight, that during his work in America he came to the gloomy conclusion that he would be a hundred and ten years of age before he could think of starting on that flight which indeed took place in 1925. He was at that time carrying on a wearying lecture tour in America in order to collect funds. The Norwegian Aero Club, with which he allied himself, would at the same time endeavor to arouse interest at home. Well acquainted as Amundsen is

COLN ELLSWORTH.

Nome. Alaska.

with these things after nearly thirty years' labor, we venture to assert with conviction that we ourselves should never have succeeded even with the most frantic efforts in bringing this enterprise to fulfillment. Ingratitude and forgetfulness seem to flourish like weeds, and there are many people who seek to belittle Ellsworth's assistance because he contributed only a part of the whole cost. "Pooh!" you hear them say, "he has really given only a third part." Yes, that is true; but we must not forget that Ellsworth's contributions to both these expeditions must be regarded as a foundation of the undertaking. Without that foundation, success could never have been achieved. We can safely say that Ellsworth's contribution of eighty-five thousand dollars in October 1924 was the foundation upon which both the flights were based. His subsequent offer of a hundred and twenty-five thousand dollars helped in the completion of the last endeavor. Let us not forget this, and let him have the full meed of thanks that he deserves.

Some time later, at a meeting in Oslo, Colonel Nobile was appointed commander of the *Norge*. A better selection could scarcely have been made. By it was secured the man who had both built *N* 1 and had flown it for a considerable time. He must know it better, surely, than any one else; and this knowledge might, of course, be of utmost importance in an expedition like ours.

First Crossing of the Polar Sea

Upon Amundsen's return from his lecture tour in America the *Norge* had her trial trip with the full Norwegian-Italian crew on board. Everything answered excellently, and everything looked promising. Ellsworth had come a few days before to meet Amundsen in Oslo, and would, with the latter, proceed by sea to Svalbard in order to take part in the many preparations that still had to be made before the *Norge* could be received there. We, however, had word that our presence in Rome was desirable. A few days after Amundsen's return from America we therefore turned southward. We arrived just in time to witness, as spectators, the *Norge* change flags from the Italian to the Norwegian. The following day we went northward again, and shortly afterwards proceeded towards Svalbard. The expedition had two vessels at its disposal. The *Knut Skaaluren* had been hired by ourselves, whilst the *Heimdal* was placed at our disposal by the State. The former could leave Tromsö about the 13th of April, the latter not before the 22nd at the earliest. It was obviously necessary that we who were to get everything ready as quickly as possible for the reception of the *Norge* should take the first boat. When we arrived at Trondhjem in the morning, in order to proceed from there by the fast route to Tromsö, the *Skaaluren* lay there. Naturally we went on board to pay Captain Jensen a visit, and at the same time to find out how many passengers he could take. It was very disheartening to learn that he could take only six, and we were fourteen. But there is always some way out of a difficulty, and in time we found room for all the fourteen, but then it was so crowded that a mouse could not have crept in anywhere! Our astonishment was great, therefore, when on going ashore again we met a smiling, corpulent, foreign scientist, who informed us that he was to go with the *Skaaluren*. We looked questioningly at each other. He realized that we were taken by surprise. "Yes," he said, "I have permission from the secretary of the Norwegian Aero Club to accompany you, and I have already taken my instruments on board." It is unpleasant to have to disappoint a man who is acting in good faith, and considers himself within his rights, but in this case there was nothing to be done. Telling him that the *Heimdal* was to leave Hammerfest about the 22nd, we left him, but it was clear that he was very disappointed.

On the 17th of April, at 1 A.M., we reached Tromsö. Here we had the great pleasure of having our old friend and companion of the previous year's expedition, Apothecary Zapffe, join us, and take over his old post as commissariat-chief, doctor, and apothecary. The same evening at eleven o'clock we left Tromsö on board the *Skaaluren*. The voyage across was uneventful; there was not even a case of sea-sickness. On the 21st, at 5 P.M., we arrived at King's Bay. A little ice alongside the coal company's wharf was all that we met with here. It was soon dispersed, and at 3 A.M. we moored alongside the wharf. How different everything was from the previous year! Then, the whole fjord lay covered with new ice, but now none was to be seen. On the other hand, there was much more snow now than last year. We saw at once we should have our work cut out in all this snow. The monument erected to commemorate the previous year's flight looked picturesque in these surroundings. It is a beautiful monolith with the names of the six who made the venture inscribed thereon. Director M. Knutsen designed it, and for this all credit is due to him. It stands on the height just above the place from where we started. Our thoughts immediately went to Commander Byrd, whom we had met a few weeks previously in New York. He had come to us at our hotel and told us of his plan to fly to the North Pole. We told him then about our experience with regard to ice-conditions at King's Bay, and expressed our sincere opinion that the ice in there would be the best place for him to make his start. And here lay the bay quite free of ice! What would Byrd think of us? Would he think that we were trying to mislead him? Although our consciences were quite clear, we discussed this matter daily, hoping the ice would form so that he could use the starting-place we had suggested to him.

Plans and Preparations

How absolutely changed New Aalesund had become. There stood the huge airship hangar, built in the course of the winter, and completely dominating all else: the houses appeared to vanish altogether in the vicinity of this colossus. And not far away stood the newly raised mooring-mast. First-Lieutenant Joh. Höver, who accompanied the *Skaaluren* in order to superintend the last preparations for the reception of the *Norge,* carried out a splendid piece of work in the fortnight intervening before we could receive the ship. As Höver had already, in the autumn of 1925, been at Svalbard to select the best place for the airship hangar and the mooring-mast, we will leave him, being best acquainted with this work, to describe these extensive and laborious preparatory operations.

JOH. HÖVER

CHAPTER TWO

The Hangar and the Mooring-Masts

CHAPTER II

THE HANGAR AND THE MOORING-MASTS

The same evening on which Roald Amundsen had delivered his lecture on the previous year's polar flight in the National Theatre, Riiser-Larsen paced restlessly to and fro in his room endeavoring to come to a decision on the question of whether he should already, the next evening, proceed to King's Bay in order to select a place for the mooring-mast which had to be erected for Amundsen's projected expedition with an airship over the Polar Sea.

In three days' time Director Brandal was to go to Svalbard with a collier-boat, and an opportunity of such a traveling-companion was not often to be found. The next day, however, brought other demands, and Riiser-Larsen instead hurriedly journeyed to Rome.

After his return from there the above-mentioned question was brought up, but now a new alternative had presented itself—namely, an airship hangar; and before it was decided which of these two could be procured or afforded it was difficult to take any steps. It was by the merest chance that I one day offered my services if they could be of any value. Riiser-Larsen's lecture tour had, in the meantime, been arranged, so that it was impossible for him to go to Svalbard. My mention of the necessary leave of absence, however, he laid quite on one side, and promptly announced it to the Norwegian Aero Club, at their general meeting, when he roughly outlined the plans for the expedition.

Then some time went by, and the funds of the expedition increased to such a degree that at the director's meeting of the Aero Club on the 22nd of September they ventured to grant *both* mast and hangar for Svalbard. I was summoned to this meeting, and was requested to go to King's Bay as soon as possible in order to make plans for the most northern airship station in the world, and, according to my own judgment, in the most favorable way known in the technicalities of aviation.

I obtained my leave of absence without delay. Of course, some preparations had to be made and some necessary things sent to Aalesund, from where the last boat of the year, belonging to the King's Bay Coal Company, was to sail early in October. The company assisted us in every possible way, and on the 4th of October the *Sörland* started, with New Aalesund, Svalbard, as her destination. Cement and steel poles were the most important shipments we took with us. The bolts for the foundation of the mooring-mast were 2 meters long and 23.5 centimeters in circumference.

It was a bad time of the year to go to Svalbard.

The Hangar and the Mooring-Masts

It had been blowing so hard in Aalesund that the discharging of coal had had to be interrupted several times, both coal and coal-trolleys being blown from their places. Storm and dirty weather steadily accompanied us also on the voyage. We took thirteen days, compared with the normal six. But, apart from a couple of dangerous situations, first outside Trondhjem Fjord and the second under Björnöen, it was extremely pleasant on board with Captain Wergeland. We had no good weather until we approached Svalbard. On the 17th of October we reached King's Bay (New Aalesund).

We called at Green Harbour also, however, in order to take on board the inspector of mines for Svalbard, Engineer Merckoll, who had to go to the King's Bay mine-field on a visit of inspection. In Green Harbour there lay Amundsen's old rival, the Algarson expedition, with the schooner *Island*. She was now to be towed home by the *Ameland,* the last boat from Green Harbour. Those on board had become weary of Algarson's leadership, and Captain Worsley and his crew had put him on one side.

The ship had lost her propeller at North-East Land on the voyage up, and had subsequently been taken, in the manner of the good old days, under sail to Franz Josef Land and back to Green Harbour. According to all reports they had discovered some new flora and some small marine animals—a Lilliputian octopus, and so on. It was now pleasant to see the vessel again; there had as a matter of fact been some rumors that the crew had taken to the oars in order to get clear of the ice.

It was a beautiful polar night that preceded the day of our arrival. The Aurora Borealis spread over the whole sky to southward, and, with the stars, it was reflected in the dead-calm sea. The next day was correspondingly beautiful. We entered King's Bay in the gray dawn, and soon were compelled to twist and turn between the masses of calf-ice from the glaciers. These can attain a height of up to six or eight meters above the water. It was a peculiarity of the year for the glaciers to calve so late, and it continued, with crashing and splitting, all the time I was up there. The approach to the harbor was one of natural beauty: the snow-covered roofed peaks, with the pyramid—or loghouse-shaped mountain-tops—Nora, Svea, and Dana (about 380 ft.)—as central figures, were remarkably beautiful against the golden-red morning sky.

At ten o'clock we landed, and, after I had called on the chief-manager, Mr. Sherdal, my own special task commenced.

In lonely silence I began my inspection of those places that, according to the map, I supposed would have to be chosen from. The only being that occasionally paid a visit to the "vagrant," whom he did not seem to care much about, was the polar dog, Jacob. This dog originates from Amundsen's

The Hangar and the Mooring-Masts

South Pole dogs, but he was obviously more cowardly, as he contented himself by watching from a distance.

At 3.30 it was dark, but I had been everywhere twice. "This is a bad lookout," thought I to myself many times as, with somewhat weary limbs, I trudged homewards, seeing in my mind's eye Pulham, Cuers, Nordholtz, and other airship stations abroad that I knew. My kind hosts, Mr. Sherdal and his wife, did not however share my impression; for they thought that there must be some sites for both hangar and mast.

I had met with the right people with whom to discuss the matter. Engineer Sherdal had been at King's Bay mines for six years, and could tell a great many things about weather conditions at King's Bay. To begin with, he had put guys and stays to the houses in the camp, so that they should not be blown away or overturned. But after a couple of years these steel wires were stowed away or turned to more profitable use. Now the houses in King's Bay are built in the same way as ours at home in East Norway, and the next airship hangar will certainly be erected in a correspondingly simplified manner.

The wind always blows, so to speak, straight out of the fjord, from the glacier called King's Highway. Occasionally it blows from the opposite direction, from north-west, and in really stormy weather from south-west, from the mountains and Brögger glaciers over the "camp"—that is, the mining-town of New Aalesund. Other directions of the wind are rare.

The subject of conversation that evening was naturally about the hangar and all connected with it, and, after having obtained favorable answers to a hundred and one questions, I then at last saw the conditions in a lighter frame of mind. I had looked on things from a too international point of view, and had been too disposed to desire to compare "my" station with those previously mentioned.

The next day (Sunday) it was still fine weather, and almost clear of snow on the ground. I was stiff after the exertions of the day before, coming suddenly after a fortnight's voyage without any particularly great exercise, but in Engineer Sherdal's agreeable company I quickly and easily went a new round of three hours. I selected the site, and Mr. Sherdal had to demonstrate and indicate the results. Thus we stepped out 300 meters here and 400 meters there, and so on, and came to the conclusion that there the one corner should be. The line to the next corner had to be made in the direction of the prevailing wind that comes from the fjord, and at the same time over some horizontal ground for a length of 120 meters. One hundred and twenty meters is a long distance in open country, especially when one must have the greatest possible distance at both ends. The hangar, which is 110 x 34 x 30 meters high, thus covers an area of three and three-quarter *maal* (a *maal* is about a quarter of an acre). Two small stone beacons now indicated the approximate positions of the south and the west corners. But this decision required thought and consideration. As far as the mast was concerned, it was still too early even to come to any temporary decision, and then darkness had fallen also.

The next day there was thick drifting snow, and the temperature remained, as before, 10° below zero, centigrade. I trudged off again to my "holy place," but this time with an assistant and a measuring-tape and theodolite. I could, however, do no more than exchange the two stone beacons for iron posts and add two more, so that the four corners were thereby marked out for the time being. On account of the snowy weather during the daytime I had two nights to sleep upon my decision.

But when Wednesday came, with clear weather and 20° below zero, centigrade, which even now did not feel cold, I found all well, and proceeded with the leveling of the ground and the marking out of the site. This was situated about 450 meters S.S.E. of the manager's residence (The Villa), with longitudinal axis about S.E. by N.W., about 20 meters above the sea-level, and nearly 300 meters from the beach.

The *Alekto*—with the master builder, Mr. Arild,

First Crossing of the Polar Sea

and twenty-one men—arrived at King's Bay at noon on Friday, the 23rd of October, after a fine voyage in moderate weather. The cargo consisted of about 600 cubic meters of timber and 50 tons of iron for the airship hangar, and also equipment, tools, and provisions for about thirty-two men for the winter. Nothing seemed to have been overlooked. The men were full of life and good-humor; this was particularly evident when they stepped ashore. Many of them were accustomed to traveling, having accompanied Arild and the foreman, Andresen, to Rio in 1922, where they put up the "Norway pavilion." "Never mind the climate," they said, who had been last in the tropics in 23° south latitude, and were now in 79° north latitude. Instead of having an after-dinner nap, most of them made off to Amundsen's commemoration stone and "the site." In the afternoon they were installed in "The Pole Barracks" and in "The Fatherland," and at 6 P.M. the discharging was in full swing. This was carried on in two shifts, from 7 A.M. to midnight, until Wednesday evening, when all the cargo had been brought on land. It was a fine haphazard sort of heap on both sides of the railway-line which indicated that the work for Amundsen's next expedition was now in full swing. We had at our disposal three small fjord horses from the King's Bay Company, but, as they were scarcely sufficient, we had already by Wednesday commenced laying a

The Hangar and the Mooring-Masts

railway-line to the site, about 400 meters from the nearest connecting-point. This, unfortunately, was not ready until the cargo had been discharged. The further transport up to the building site had then to be taken as an operation by itself. The whole of the discharging proceeded in the finest winter weather, and prospects that the weather would hold were of the best.

Whilst the *Alekto* on Thursday took in coal and water, I put the finishing touch to my task and marked out a place for the foundation of the mast. With his well-equipped expedition and excellent assistance the master builder Arild obtained in the well-supplied workshops and warehouses belonging to the King's Bay Company, and also with the kindness and help shown to us, I had good trust in all being ready at the right time, unless the weather became too unreasonable. Shoveling snow on the scene of operations may, as a matter of fact, be a very troublesome evil. Carpenters and cement-workers had quite enough to do. The skeleton of the hangar had to be erected, and all foundation work, as well as the casting of the anchoring-blocks of the mooring-mast and the hangar—in all 200 cubic meters of concrete-casting—had to be finished by April. This was necessary in order that the mast itself and the canvas covering of the hangar might be erected in good time.

An incalculably great advantage to the work, and

a great benefit for all the inhabitants of the camp, was the fact that the Aero Club had at its disposal the power-station of the company. Of what value it will be to have the electric light during the four long, dark months! Another thing that is dependent on electric power is the newly constructed water supply plant. This is new and peculiar of its kind, and very ingeniously constructed. Previously, water has been carted to the camp from Tvillings Lake, which has the peculiarity of not freezing entirely to the bottom owing to the warm spring. Otherwise it has been necessary to obtain water by melting snow and ice. Last summer, however, they took definite steps, and laid a pump main for the remaining two kilometers. The insulation, which consists of white moss and hay doubly encysted, is so good that when, at 20° below zero, centigrade, one used 4 kilowatts through an insulated conductor along the pipe itself, then one got the whole power back as increase of temperature in the water from 1° to 4° above zero.

When the Aero Club thus, by working the power-station, procured light and water for themselves and for the others who were wintering there, it can be understood why they got the good reputation that they did.

During their winter residence there our people—thirty-two men in all—would scarcely suffer. But conditions are represented as much worse than they

The Hangar and the Mooring-Masts

really are as experienced on the spot. It would be, however, a rough job to carry out such constructive work during the polar night. Rough heavy beams of up to 20 x 30 centimeters are no joke when they are, besides, slippery and difficult to handle on account of ice and snow. Still, all was carried out with great precision, and entirely according to the program. On the 15th of February 1926, the skeleton of this proud building was raised, and the flag waved from the top, as is the custom in Norway when the top of a building is reached. About 27 kilometers of beams were used for this work. The hangar consists in all of twenty-three pairs of such trestles. The foundation girders should really have been rectangular, but as it was hopeless to think of getting the ground leveled in the time at our disposal, we promptly changed the form of the girders so that the bottom beams followed the general contour of the ground. It will be interesting to learn how so superficial a building stands in the thaw and in the new ice-forming time. The ground is as favorable as possible, so it will certainly stand for a time. It has, in any case, done full service.

Freia chocolate factory, Tidemann and others—who this time showed their generosity—assisted also in making the best possible conditions.

When the *Alekto,* on the 30th of October, left New Aalesund, it was stated that it was the latest date of departure for a cargo-boat or any large vessel. On the 26th the sun disappears in New Aalesund. To compensate for this, the moon is always up, and keeps above the horizon all the twenty-four hours. We had, therefore, no difficulty in coming out of the fjord, which was as free of ice as in the middle of summer. We had summer weather the whole voyage over the Arctic. It was clear, and there were even degrees of heat as soon as we got free of the land, but in Norway it was winter.

With short interruptions, the good weather continued in New Aalesund for a fairly long time. Heavy railway-trains, with two to four trucks, plied night and day for a week, and the work of raising the base framework was commenced. The buckles were here constructed together in two halves, the under and upper each by itself. Towards Christmas the girders were laid and the erecting of the underpart could begin.

All went absolutely according to program, and Mr. Arild and the carpenters deserve great praise. Little by little, as the base framework disappeared in the snow, the hangar rose in the air. Neither gale nor 35° of frost were capable of hindering us. But the snow was sometimes troublesome in concealing the materials; even the shed was difficult to find again after a snowstorm, with heavy drift, which we experienced at the beginning of February, although it had a gable height of 7 meters.

The Hangar and the Mooring-Masts

At the same time as the carpenters' work at the hangar was going on, the making of the concrete anchoring-blocks for the mooring-mast proceeded. This is triangular in shape, with a 6-meter base, and is fastened at each corner to a 40-ton concrete block, furnished with the already-mentioned heavy steel bolts, which Nylands' works forged for us. The Coal Company had previously carried on the concrete-casting the whole winter, and, with the experience therefrom, this work also went on smartly and well. Blasting in frost is a work of patience, and much ammunition is required. There was good sand on the beach a few hundred meters away, and "percentage stones" in the refuse-heaps from the mines. There was also hot water in the boilers of the power-station, as well as 30,000 tons of coal to take from for the heating of sand and stone.

By Christmas the foundations of the mast were finished, and then came the turn for the sixteen large backstays of the hangar. This was an equally great task, which proceeded with the same speed and precision as the raising of the hangar. A great deal of forge work had, therefore, to be done over again on account of the changing of the original girders. Thanks to the large stock of ironbolting belonging to the Coal Company, we did not run short. Engineer Smith-Meyer looked with dismay at his diminishing store!

As soon as everything was ready to receive the

covering of the hangar and the mooring-mast, the working party took a well-earned rest for a week.

It was the well-known *Hobby*—Captain Holm—which now appeared to have become the expedition-vessel most in request, for this year she was the first up north. Holm is the type of genial and skillful seaman. Although young, he is himself an ice-pilot, and the vessel is strong as a mountain; but the motor is not excessively powerful, yet Holm always gets to the spot in good time.

In Trondhjem the *Hobby* loaded up some materials, some provisions, petrol, and oil, and then finally the canvas (French hangar-cloth), of about ten thousand square meters (two and a half acres), which was to cover the sides and gables of the hangar. This was no trifle which the sailmaker, Houdan, had in a short time put together. Furnished with bolt-ropes, eyes, and hanks, like a sail of the good old days, the walls consisted of twenty-two such "patches" of thirty by thirty-two by five meters. Every piece covered the intervening space between the beams, and was laced fast to these. This required many kilometers of cord. The "doors," or gable walls, were absolute monsters. With one piece an opening of about thirty by twenty-four meters had to be covered. As the wind-screen and strain on the wooden construction would be much too great in a storm if these curtains were flat like another topsail, they were given the form of a half-pyramid, with the top on the ground about twenty-five meters out from the wall. They were fastened to the walls themselves with iron bands and running-gear that went quite to the top. The hoisting was effected by a winch on each side.

On the 9th of March the *Cygnus* came from Italy to Trondhjem, a week delayed, with all the aviation equipment, hydrogen cylinders, and mooring-mast, and also with a mast and its equipment for Vadsö. Of all these things it was more particularly the mooring-masts and hangar-cloth that demanded to be dealt with immediately. According to the original plan the things should have been in Trondhjem a fortnight earlier, so that there was no time to lose. The three largest shipments for the mooring-mast were the lower part of the corner-beams, with their length of 16.5 meters and weight of 1.5 tons. These were somewhat difficult to handle on a rather small vessel, but all went well. It was a compensation to find that all the 140 cases were excellently packed: the weight of each case was as far as possible kept to 200 kilograms. It varied somewhat, however, from 50 kilograms for the case with reserve gas-valves to 650 kilograms for motors and reserve rudder-blades, which were the heaviest; but, as far as these last were concerned, the packing weighed eight times as much as the objects themselves. There were altogether 29 tons of such goods. The remainder of the cargo of the *Hobby* amounted to 140 tons, which represented 900 hydrogen cylinders. Each such cylinder weighs, as a matter of fact, about 160 kilograms. With a volume of 100 liters and filled to 100 atmospheres, they took up 10 cubic meters of hydrogen gas of 1 atmosphere pressure.

When, on the 24th of March, the *Hobby* arrived at New Aalesund, where it was still quite free of ice, work was renewed with vigor. In the shortest possible time the hangar had to be covered with canvas, and the mast erected.

There were in the meantime also other places in Norway where intense labor was going on for receiving the airship *Norge*. When it had been decided that the route should be taken by way of Oslo and North Norway, I got a request from the Aero Club in January to proceed to North Norway in order to find a place for a mooring-mast there. Nyborgmoen had been fixed upon as a likely place if it could be found practicable.

In the meantime Riiser-Larsen had selected Ekeberg Flats for a mast at Oslo, and the work on the ground soon began there. On the 21st of January I went northward, and, after a fortnight's inspection of the stretch between Harstad and Kirkeness, I fixed on Vadsöy, outside the town of Vadsö, as the one most suitable in all respects for a mooring-mast. The meteorologists certainly gave a word of

The Hangar and the Mooring-Masts

warning against this place, but, after having studied Mr. H. Esbensen's journals regarding the weather conditions in April and May during the last five years, and also *Atlas's* log for two years, I found no reason to choose any other place than Vadsöy, where the conditions of the ground were the most favorable. I am greatly obliged to Mr. Esbensen for the access to his journals and for the great service they afforded me. The selected area, which belonged to the municipality, was very readily placed at my disposal by the corporation.

I was also fortunate to at once find a man—Chief Engineer Fixdal—who was willing to undertake all the work of raising and mounting the mast. The result proved that he, with the assistance of Kværner Mills, did it well and successfully in every way. The Italian engineer, Rossi—who later on came to Vadsö to mount and to attend to the supply arrangements for the gas, petrol, and ballast at the mast according to the Italian system, also received further benefit from Mr. Fixdal's judgment.

The mast, with its appurtenances, arrived at Vadsö from Italy on the 26th of March, and all was ready for use on the 26th of April.

The Oslo mast had, in the meantime, been constructed by the Kværner Mills by Engineer Roll on the basis of the Italian designs. The available materials, however, were used, and for this reason the details were much altered. The mast was raised in no time, but, as the mast-head itself, with swivel and mooring-cone, had to be borrowed from Rome, it was not entirely ready until the last moment. Busy were the days that preceded the arrival of the *Norge* at Oslo on the 14th of April.

"You must be chief of the station at Spitsbergen in the spring," said Riiser-Larsen, when I came home to Oslo after having been at Svalbard in October. "And so you *must* come to Rome when the trial flights begin in order to learn how to handle the airship on the ground, in and out of the hangar, and to and from the mooring-mast."

"That would be quite interesting if only I could get leave," I replied.

But I heard no more of this matter until I came back from Finmark on the 12th of February. Then I got a request from the Aero Club to proceed to Rome for the purpose mentioned. The original intention had been that I should go with the first boat to Svalbard in order to mount the mast there. As before mentioned it was sent by the *Hobby*. But, as the alterations in the airship and the trial flights had also been somewhat delayed, this was not possible. Engineer Diderich Lund got this commission, and Colonel Nobile sent one of his engineers, Major Rossi, to Vadsö.

On my return there was little opportunity for any instruction in mast equipment at Oslo. We had a trial with the detachment of the Guard Regiment that was to assist with the mooring, and when some Italian mechanics arrived to take charge of the gas-filling arrangement the time came to go northwards from Oslo.

It was the *Knut Skaaluren* which was freighted for New Aalesund with the remaining 3,900 hydrogen cylinders (625 tons) and with the equipment and provisions of the expedition.

On the same day on which the *Skaaluren* left Tromsö the covering of the hangar (at King's Bay) with canvas was completed, and the landscape looked quite different. Engineer Lund, with the available hands, had also in a week succeeded in putting together the mast to its full length as it lay on the ground.

It was by far the easiest method of putting it together; but it might prove difficult to raise such a heavy object—35 meters long, and weighing 14 tons. I had thought of this possibility when I laid the foundations, and, with this in view, had directed the base against a heavy rock (the only one) in the ground. It succeeded.

With his sober accuracy for calculation, and the use of all his ingenuity, Engineer Lund had succeeded, by means of tackle, men, and mine-winches, in raising the mast when complete. This saved at least fourteen days.

First Crossing of the Polar Sea

It was time for me and my two Norwegian and four Italian mechanics to get to work with the mounting of the fixtures for the mast, and also later the making ready of the hangar. For this work a fortnight had been estimated, but, had we not lost several working days on account of snow-storms we could have completed it in less time. At this time we had also transported 360 gas cylinders and everything belonging to the mast, as well as 2,800 cylinders for the reserve parts. In praise of Colonel Nobile and his assistants it must be said that there was nothing lacking. There was rather, indeed, a little too much. We who were acquainted with conditions at Svalbard during the summer season could not help smiling when it was found that on the list of things packed there had also been sent flashlights, motor generators, and lamps, etc.—that is to say, a full equipment for the illumination of the hangar and the landing-place for landing in the dark.

In all, nearly 2,000 tons of cargo were conveyed in connection with the expedition of 1926.

ROALD AMUNDSEN AND
LINCOLN ELLSWORTH

Waiting at Svalbard

CHAPTER III

It does not often happen that one is awakened by music in Svalbard, but at any rate this happened on Sunday, the 25th of April. It was a marvelously beautiful morning; all was brilliantly clear and still. We were not exactly awakened, for we lay enjoying the delightful view of the pure white hills and the fresh air coming in through the open windows. There was a spirit of festivity in the air. , Suddenly one of the well-known hymn-tunes reached us. We knew at once that it was the *Heimdal,* with her military band. We quickly got into our clothes and went out. There she lay alongside the quay, and the passengers and sailors were already sight-seeing in New Aalesund. Captain Tank-Nielsen had had a good voyage, and had not been hindered by ice. It was a relief to know the *Heimdal* was on the spot, for now we should get assistance from the many lads on board. The chief task was the clearing away of the snow. The long railway-line must be brought to light before traffic could be got into good going order. But this was no easy task. In places there lay as much as two meters of hard-pressed snow over the line, and it was heavy work to shovel this away. Still it went on, and all went well. It could not be expected that it would vanish like dew before the rays of the sun, for hard-pressed snow is considerably more difficult to deal with than dew. Thus it took us fourteen days to get all in order, but when everything is taken into consideration it was quickly done.

On the 29th of April the American steamer *Chantier* arrived, with the members of the Byrd expedition. As mentioned before, we had recently talked with Byrd at the Waldorf Astoria Hotel in New York, where he had told us all about his plans. It is by no means the case—as so many newspapers have asserted—that this meeting was a complete surprise, and that the intention of Byrd's flight to the Pole was to get there first. We knew all the details of his plans, and we not only gave him our sympathy, but offered all the assistance we could afford him. We venture to say that our intercourse at Svalbard was marked by the greatest good will towards each other, a feeling that has later resulted in friendship. Byrd had a hard time to go through at the beginning. The *Heimdal* had occupied the only little bit of quay that was to be found, and was busy taking in coal and water when the *Chantier* arrived. She had to do this so as to be ready for the time when the *Norge* left Leningrad, so that in case anything happened she could go out and offer assistance. There was also something wrong with one

of the boilers, and this made it still further necessary for Captain Tank-Nielsen to refuse Byrd when
he asked for the place at the quay. This was a pity,
and might, at first glance, seem that we were ill disposed, but the good Americans understood. The
Chantier thereupon went in alongside the *Heimdal*
and moored. Commander Byrd at once paid us a
visit at our residence at New Aalesund, and shortly
afterwards we went on board the *Chantier*. Here
we experienced something quite novel. Everything
had been presented as gifts; all were volunteers.
Think what a country to work in! Immediately we
got on board we passed a man who was dreadfully
grimy. We both seemed to have some recollection
of him. We stopped and asked him if we had not
met before. "Oh, yes," he answered, with a peal of
laughter; "I am employed in the X bank in New
York, and we have met there several times." The
crew consisted, for the most part, of such people;
they had all joined full of enthusiasm for the enterprise; here was no worrying about money or
fame, but only to go forward. We understood soon
enough that it would take more than ice or snow
to stop these fellows. Relations on board were
splendid, and we could clearly see how much this
quiet, calm commander was esteemed and respected.

The day after, the *Hobby*, our old friend of the
previous year, arrived. She was to assist the Byrd
expedition. On the 1st of May, this curiously com-

pounded crew executed a piece of work that we—who were on the spot and saw it—will always remember with respect and admiration. As it took a longer time than expected with the *Heimdal's* work at the quay, Byrd determined to take his aeroplane ashore through the drift-ice, which at this time had drifted in and lay round the *Chantier*. The undertaking was extremely hazardous, but was carried out with a power and judgment that forced us all to the highest point of admiration. Four lifeboats were lashed together, and then the big Fokker machine was lowered down on to the top of them. Involuntarily we all held our breath. Through the current and drifting ice this raft was then brought to the shore. It sounds so easy, but it must be borne in mind that every inch meant imminent danger to the whole transport. Everything was staked on one card, and—they won. Amidst loud cheering they reached the shore, and in a phenomenally short time the *Josephine Ford* (the name of the aeroplane) was beached. There was obviously nothing that could stop these fellows. Now began an immense activity night and day. They could not, it was clear, take off from the ice as we had done the previous year, but had to find a land track. After very careful investigation of the ground, they decided on the piece just above, and a little to the right of, our hangar. The slope here was quite gentle, and the ground fairly even for ordinary purposes.

Waiting at Svalbard

But for those who were to fly off from here there was much to do. Day by day the snow was trampled and leveled. It was interesting to follow this work. We could not help thinking of busy ants. It was a matter of course that these people liked to have their operations photographed. They had also a huge staff of photographers, both for moving pictures and others. There was, however, a regulation inside our area that no outsider should take photographs, and the Byrd expedition was really right in the center of our area. This was a disagreeable business, and it often annoyed me. We solved the problem, however, in this way: we came to an agreement that they should only photograph their work and we ours. But before this arrangement had come into force we can remember how one of the photographers of the Byrd expedition had taken up his position on drift-ice, and from there had taken all the photographs he wished. Besides, from the *Chantier,* with their telephoto lenses, they could take what photographs they liked. The regulation was thus quite a *pro forma* one, in order to protect ourselves against the newspapers and journals we had contracted with. Later on nobody troubled about this regulation, which in reality was impossible to keep. A photographer will, in some way or other, sneak in to get what he cannot have with good will. We can, for instance, recall our own photographer prowling about all hours of the day and night round

Byrd's forbidden people, trying to photograph them and their work in the most unbelievable ways. If one suddenly came round a corner one could often see the legs of a photographer's tripod disappear into the first available hiding-place! Berge can boast that he was the only film-photographer on the spot when Byrd returned from the Pole.

On the 3rd of May the first trial was made, but they had the misfortune to break a ski. This happened again the second time, and it really began to look doubtful if they would succeed in getting up at all. But here, as in everything else, their ingenuity and perseverance won the day, and at last they could rejoice in having solid landing-gear. The track also became better and better, and finally looked like a skating-rink.

At last we could send the "ready" telegram to the *Norge* at Leningrad, and on the 5th we received the announcement that she had left that place at 9.30 A.M. Here came the most exciting part of the *Norge's* flight—from Leningrad over Vadsö to Svalbard. It went so far that several experts had expressed their conviction that when the flight to Svalbard was accomplished the whole flight was really over; that the flight over the Polar Sea was quite simple in comparison. One may ask oneself what grounds they had for this statement. Certainly not experience. But what, then? Presumably they wished to calm the minds of their fellow-men. For we who went northward by steamer this remark of theirs was very unfortunate. We can still remember the mistrustful glances, and even words, that were sent after us: "Why are you not on board now, when the most difficult part is to be crossed?" This was quite ridiculous, but quite a natural result of the statements given above.

On the 6th, we received a telegram from First-Lieutenant Svend Brun, our valuable assistant in Vadsö, that the *Norge* had moored to the mast at 6 A.M., and was expected to proceed northwards in a few hours. King's Bay wireless station, which was the whole time in the service of the expedition under Telegraphist Mörk's supervision, had been invaluable to us. It picked up, for instance, telegrams from the *Norge* from the most diverse places on the route, and kept us informed. Thus its communication with Björnöen was heard, and also Björnöen's reports. During the flight over the sea we had a high barometer, light easterly breeze, some snow, and not very good visibility. There was not much rest to be had on the night before the 7th. There was continual traffic between our house and the telegraph station. At 5 A.M. Olonkin telegraphed and said they were now right over the fjord mouth. The alarm was then sounded for all men to be at their posts in order to receive and conduct the *Norge* into the hangar. The day before all of them had been divided into parties and instructed by Lieutenant Höver.

How we stared and stared! It was a splendid morning, clear and still. The smoke from our pipes went straight up, without so much as an attempt to curve to one side or the other. On the landing-place, a little below the hangar, there were swarms of people. The *Heimdal's* crew and the carpenters, together with all the Italian workmen, were busy getting into their allotted places. Orders were shouted through huge megaphones; one moment it was Lieutenant Höver in Norwegian, then Major Vallini in Italian, then both at once without anybody understanding. Order was restored after a while, and when at last the *Norge* came in sight outside Cape Mitra the V-formation was ready. The *Norge* was not an impressive sight at first—merely a little dark speck which could scarcely be seen to move; but the speck became larger, and began by degrees to take the shape of what was the first dirigible airship in these regions. The excitement amongst the waiting crowd increased as the *Norge* approached and assumed larger and larger dimensions. Yet nothing can be called really large in this colossal environment, for Nature herself takes command and plays the principal part. Everything seems small in this wonderful scenery.

After flying in circles over the place—probably to get acquainted with the conditions—the airship slowly and quietly sank down towards the assistants on the ground. The maneuver was fine, and made a strong impression on us. The man who was in command seemed to understand his job. At 6 A.M. the mooring-line whizzed out from the *Norge,* and immediately afterwards was in the safe keeping of hundreds of strong hands. She was hauled right down to the ground. It was absolutely still, and there was no reason to be anxious about surprises of any kind. There was now a universal scene of mutual recognition. From the windows of the airship peeped out familiar faces, and in all three motor-gondolas the mechanics were seen moving about like monkeys. "Oh, good morning, good morning, Horgen" ("*Morgen, Horgen*"), is shouted cheerily. It is Apothecary Zapffe, who, from amongst the spectators, welcomes his friend First-Lieutenant Horgen, who is in the steering gondola. But the latter was not without his ready answer: "Good day, good day, *Za(p)ffe.* Shall we soon *skaffe* [1]?" Universal delight along the whole line. The ship is led to the hangar, and in the course of only a short time she is housed. All who have seen the hangar at King's Bay have been impressed and astonished; it is a great work, accomplished under more difficult conditions than any under which such a building has ever before been erected. It was built in the darkness and the cold of the Arctic

[1] Eat.

night. The head carpenter, Arild, who supervised the work, and all his men deserve the highest praise.

As soon as the airship had been brought well in we gave them all the well-earned three-times-three cheer and the band played the four national anthems—Norwegian, American, Italian, and Swedish—and then the ceremonial festivities were over. As soon as the gondola door was opened we hastened over to bid our comrades welcome. We thanked Nobile for his skillful piloting, and congratulated him upon the splendid qualities the *Norge* had displayed. It was pleasant to see all the old faces again; they all looked well and fresh. One thing, however, struck us at once—they shivered and froze and begged to get into the house as quickly as possible and have some warm coffee. It was no wonder that they froze, dressed as they were in quite ordinary sports suits, as if they were going for a summer picnic in the woods! We expressed our surprise at this, and asked the reason, but we could not get any satisfactory answer. It is quite certain that these frozen fliers will never forget the cup of strong, boiling hot coffee our two excellent housekeepers, Berta and Klara, had in readiness for them as soon as they came into the warm, bright mess.

Questions and answers rained down.

But let us allow one of them who went the whole way from Rome to Svalbard to give us an account of the journey.

GUSTAV AMUNDSEN

CHAPTER FOUR

From Rome to Svalbard

CHAPTER IV

Many people have often asked me why I have not taken part in any of my uncle's expeditions. The same answer has had to be given to them all: that he is unwilling to have members of his family with him. Still I have made the most earnest endeavors from time to time to accompany him, but always unsuccessfully. I was not a very big fellow the first time I asked to go, as his answer tends to show: "Go home and eat more porridge and then we will talk about it." The next time I asked, I went to work more diplomatically, as I induced my father to go into the firing-line, but the result he attained put a check for all time on any further attempt. "I will not agree to have any relations on such expeditions, where we are on board the same vessel for ages. The consequences are too big"; and in my heart I had to admit he was right. My part in the future was therefore that of spectator. I was with him, heart and soul, the whole time, but, unfortunately, only passive.

Until last summer—that is. The members of last year's expedition, some naval officers and the nearest relations to Roald Amundsen met at Uranienborg. After dinner we all sat chatting on the verandah steps, and some photographs were taken. Suddenly I heard Riiser-Larsen say, "Lend me your camera a moment," and thereupon he took a photograph of the four of us who were sitting on the steps—I do not quite remember who they were now, but that I was one of them is certain. After having snapped us, Riiser-Larsen then said, "Yes, now I have taken the four quartermasters of the *Norge*." I did not attach much importance to this remark and thought it referred to something the others had amongst themselves from the past year's Svalbard tour, but when a moment later I went up the steps, and into the house, I passed Riiser-Larsen sitting with my mother, engaged in a very serious conversation, and as I went past he looked at me smilingly: "Well, what do you say to being with us?" At first I did not understand. "Who be with you? and where?" "You, of course, as streersman on the airship next year." If the lightning had struck just in front of me, I could scarcely have been more astonished, and after surprise came joy—wild and unrestrained—but it soon came to an end. Thoughts came and put a stop to it— thoughts of my earlier fruitless attempts to be with them, and of the last answer I received. On my earnest enquiry if the matter had been laid before the "chief," I got the answer, "No," and my hopes sank far below zero at once. But Riiser-

From Rome to Svalbard

Larsen was a man of action: "I will tackle him now," and down the steps he went. A moment after I saw the "chief" and the second-in-command standing a little away in serious conference. I must say I followed their conversation with rapt attention. It was impossible to hear what was said, but the expression on their faces told much. I can safely say it was the most exciting moment I had ever experienced. At last! . . . They were coming back. I tried to guess my fate from their expressions, but they were both equally serious. I felt like a prisoner awaiting his sentence—guilty or not guilty? I came to myself on hearing Riiser-Larsen's calm voice, "It is all in order."

In the evening when we were going to bed I took the opportunity of thanking my uncle for my being engaged, and he then answered me: "You know my principles as regards having my relations on my expeditions, but if Riiser-Larsen has engaged you then all is well."

That was the way in which I came to be appointed to the *Norge* as steersman. The whole autumn I went rejoicing, and prepared myself for being taken on the great venture. Many of my acquaintances there were who chaffed me and asked if I were mad; if I wished to make an end of myself, and so on without end!

Others again enquired: "Why will you go with them? What is your object?" To the former question it was unnecessary to answer, but to the latter I replied that in my case as well as in that of the many others who went on such exploits it is the adventure that for the most part attracts us, that longing for adventure that lies latent in us all, right from the days of childhood and onward through life. Ambition, true enough, plays a great part, for we are only human after all, but I believe the chief force that drives us on is desire for adventure, that which is so strong that it puts its hand over the humdrum tasks of daily life and the dullness of the office-stool. It was not easy indeed in these times to hold firmly to this faith altogether, on account of all those doubters; but, thanks to the good moral support my wife afforded me and the sight of the preparations for the expedition, which towards the end of the autumn began to push forward, I stood firm and steadfast.

On the 1st of January, 1926, I commenced work. Lieutenant Horgen had already for some time been occupied in preparations and my first task was then to help him.

It proved there were altogether seventeen of us engaged for the expedition, and as we occasionally heard rumors that it was quite impossible to take more than sixteen on the flight, I, who was No. 17, began, naturally enough, to be anxious about my position.

This anxiety unfortunately became a certainty

after the visit of the then Colonel Nobile to Oslo, for he would not have more than sixteen men from Svalbard, on account of the weight, and I had to be satisfied with being appointed reserve-flier. I could very well be with them to Svalbard, but further— time would only show.

It was not easy for me to come to a decision this time. Should I accompany them on the risky tour from Rome to Svalbard with the possibility of being put on shore there? Or should I take the chance in the hope that when we were once at Svalbard with the *Norge,* and the final flight should begin, there might then after all be roo.n for me?

I took the chance and, in spite of having experienced the greatest disappointment of my life, I do not regret it for a moment.

Towards the end of the autumn and onwards, work on alterations in the airship had been proceeding in Rome, and the intention then was that all we Norwegians should go there as soon as the ship was reported ready for its trial flight, in order to get the practice we needed. None of us were really expert in handling airships except Riiser-Larsen, who had gone through a course in England, so the time was short.

At the beginning of February, the first batch went to Rome, and at the close of the month we were all there except Gottwaldt and Malmgren, who both came at the beginning of March. We were all quartered in the same hotel in Rome—or perhaps it would better be called boarding-house—where we formed a little colony to ourselves. The very first day we were there we went to the factory and called on Colonel Nobile, who gave us a friendly welcome at his office. Airships are designed, the plans drawn, and the fixed parts built at the factories in Rome. The mounting itself takes place out at the huge hangar at Ciampino, about three quarters of an hour by motor car from town. Later we had the opportunity of seeing how this mounting operation for these semi-rigid airships is done; for the mounting of a military airship built by order for Japan was commenced whilst we were still there, and proceeded rapidly.

As mentioned before, the ready parts of the rigid keel came from the factory in Rome, and when the balloon itself had been inflated with gas the connecting of the frames and the keel appeared to be very simple. It was, as a matter of fact, an operation requiring great precision, and was executed by the best people procurable. In the evening of the same day on which we arrived we motored out to have a look at N 1, as the ship was then called. "Motored" is perhaps a mild description judging from our standpoint at home! I should perhaps rather say flew, but the happy medium is always best, so I will correct myself by saying we took something between a flying-trip and a motor-trip. I reckoned our speed to be about seventy or eighty kilometers an hour. It is rather fascinating to rush along a straight country road at a dizzying speed. I might perhaps say it is tempting, in any case for the driver; but for the passengers it was really less inveigling—especially under such conditions as later on were often the case, with twelve to fourteen passengers in a motor-lorry. We had by that time also given names to the different chauffeurs, who were doing their level best to bring our young lives to an early close. There were, for instance, "Lightning chauffeur" and "Lightning chauffeur's sub," amongst many others. I think indeed it would be a beneficial course of treatment for one who does not pay particular attention to the laws about speed-limit to take such a trip along the Via Appia.

My first introduction to N 1 was, I must admit, a disappointment. As a matter of fact, I thought it was small (which it scarcely could be with its length of 106 meters), but the explanation, on the whole, was the immense dimensions of the hangar. I could almost say that away in a corner was a Zeppelin, but that is really something of an exaggeration. When I say, however, that the hangar contained, besides N 1, a Zeppelin, *Esperia,* taken over from Germany after the war, and also the little airship *Mr* 1, then I am at all events not departing from the truth. The fact that about thirty men had spread out the balloon-covering for the Japanese airship I have mentioned is scarcely worth talking about, so trifling was its effect amid such surroundings.

Our ship itself had the appearance of being very unready. My thoughts flew to descriptions in the newspapers of a visit to an exhibition just before its opening: "All went on in the wildest chaos, painters and artisans everywhere, but still, at the time appointed, all was in proper order." So also here; everywhere on board there were riggers, painters, and motor-mechanics, all in apparently the most delightful confusion, but that there was method in the madness was soon apparent, and that pretty soon, for honest work went on constantly, and the ship was completed at the correct time.

Whilst the work proceeded on the ship, we worked in the city, attending a number of lectures by the then Captain Valeini, on the maneuvering of airships, which were instructive. Moreover we learnt to understand how fragile such a giant is and how little it can bear if not handled in the right way.

The intervals between the lectures we passed like schoolboys with "throwing at sticks" amongst other things, something that a Press-photographer took to be *gefundenes Fressen*, and some days later we graced one of the illustrated journals in the most remarkable attitudes, whilst we were supposed to be playing "one of our national games." We had plenty of spare time whilst waiting for the *N 1* to be ready for her trial flight.

From Rome to Svalbard

I think I can safely say that we all used this spare time well, exploring the city and all the wonderful treasures of bygone days. In the meantime tests at Ciampino went on briskly. At one lifting test it proved that the ship could lift 750 kilograms more than fixed in the contract, and my hopes of being with them on the final trip rose, only to be dashed to the ground again. More people? Not a bit of it— but two new petrol tanks.

The Norwegian Minister in Rome, Mr. Irgens, gave us a kind reception one day, and promised to procure us an audience with the Pope; a promise he later fulfilled. Our meeting with the Pope was an unforgettable red-letter day and made a great impression on us.

On the 26th of February we received word that *N* I was ready for her trial flight the following day, and that we were to be ready for departure from our boarding-house at 6 A.M. On the morning of the same day we saw the *Esperia* flying over Rome. It was a fine and imposing sight and we looked forward to the next day. The only question was, What would the weather be like? The day came with ideal flying weather, so when we turned out at 5 A.M. we were all in high feather. At 6 A.M. the car arrived and we drove at break-neck speed to Ciampino. Here it swarmed with film-Pressmen, officers, soldiers, and spectators in fine confusion. All were asking questions and fussing about. The cameras clicked incessantly, and all was pretty lively. At 9 o'clock the detachment of about 200 men that should lead the ship out of the hangar arrived. They seized hold of the maneuvering-ropes and, at the word of command from the officers in charge, the colossus then began slowly to glide out of the hangar.

Immediately before, Lieutenant Horgen and I had word from Colonel Nobile that as he, on this day, was going to have a large number of people belonging to the factory on board, it looked improbable that we would go too. Well, that was not a pleasant message to receive, but fortunately everything turned out all right, for just before the start, after the ship had been weighed, we were both called on board. We were not slow in obeying the order. At 10 o'clock we let go and rose swiftly and elegantly to about 150 meters. The motors were then started and the course set for Rome.

Most of us had previously been up in a flying-machine, but this was something quite different. Quietly and steadily we rose, and quietly and steadily we sped along.

We numbered twenty-five men on board at the trial trip, including the crew, scientific people, and journalists. The weather was beautifully clear and calm.

Immediately after rising we got something of a fright, as all the gas-pressure gauges rose far above the maximum allowed. One of our boys then re-marked quite consolingly: "If she does not burst now, she will never burst." With the earth about 200 meters below us, I must admit that I really did not relish the prospects of our immediate future very much. Fortunately it proved that the pressure-gauges had in some way stuck.

After circling over Rome, where the tourists on the cupola of St. Peter's looked enviously at us, we set our course towards the Mediterranean. When well out over it, we steered southwards along the coast and down to Naples. I had seen Naples before and had not succumbed, and the same this time, but it must be admitted that the sight from the air is far more beautiful than from the sea.

After having turned her nose a little way in over the quays, we turned and steered the *Norge* north-wards again. In the distance we saw Capri. The sea lay calm and blue beneath us, and here and there we saw a few fishermen with their boats and their remarkable rigging lying drifting. Now and then we could also see some large fish swimming lazily in the clear water.

At 5 P.M. we passed in over the land with course set for Ciampino, but first we made one more circle over Rome, and after having circled three times over the flying-ground we landed safely at 6.30 P.M. after a successful and interesting trip.

We got an opportunity, even this first day, of

training on the food allowed for the later flight, as all we Norwegians got only one cup of dreadful coffee from 6 A.M. until 8 P.M.

From now onwards we seriously began our special work, and as a rule visited the flying-ground every day. Everything depended on the weather, for if it blew ever so little there was no question of taking the ship out, as they were afraid that it might, in a light wind, get the better of the landing-party. This happened once. A gust of wind caught the ship as the bow was about to pass through the door, and she collided with it. The shock was almost unnoticeable to us who were on board, but when we got the ship out on to the ground to inspect the damage it proved that some rudder portions in the bow had been sprung, and that in addition some of the outer covering had been ripped to pieces. Colonel Nobile would not therefore undertake any flying until this damage, inconsiderable in itself, had been repaired.

We all agreed with him: one can never tell. The damage was, however, repaired and in proper order by the same evening. It was a pity that the accident happened, because the program of our practice for that day was on a large scale—first mooring practice to the mast, then a "landing" on the sea, and finally a night flight.

Unfortunately all this had to be given up, but we consoled ourselves that we still had this in store.

From Rome to Svalbard

We had had practice in mooring to the mast some days before, the landing-party having drawn the ship away to the mast, where the bow-cable was coupled up and afterwards we slackened up to 250 meters high, and then hauled down to the mast and moored. From here the ship was again hauled down to the ground and from there drawn into the hangar. It was, so far as I know, the first time an airship had been moored to a mast in Italy. The mast, which stood out on the flying-ground in the vicinity of the hangar, was specially made for the occasion.

We also had such mooring-practice once more before we undertook a complete and independent mooring. It is an ill wind that blows nobody any good, for the day after the accident with the ship, there blew a storm from the north which was so strong that we could scarcely have managed to fight against it, therefore it would not be difficult to say how long we should have been compelled to keep afloat, had we sailed. In any case, the wind continued for three days, so the prospects of landing might have been indefinite.

There was much waiting about at this time, so we agreed with the following heartfelt sigh from one of the boys: "Yes, now I can understand why those at home often call a flying institution a waiting institution."

The ship was now almost ready, with the exception of the wireless cabinet—but here also the work proceeded briskly. The engineer sent down by the Marconi Company, along with Captain Gottwaldt, worked the whole day long; and on board there only remained the mounting of some lamps and so on.

On the 9th of March at 8 P.M., *N* 1 started on her first night flight. We Norwegians were not all aboard her, so those of us who returned to Rome in the evening had an unforgettable and wonderful sight as the great silver ship came over, with its slender hull outlined against the night sky in a sea of light from the city.

Next morning at 6.30 we were again out at the flying-ground, and at 7 o'clock *N* 1 came back and was first moored to the mast and later drawn into the hangar. It had been a splendid trip, and one with which all were more than satisfied. It was fairly cold and there was little sleep to be had— otherwise everything was all right.

After this trip there was a long interval of waiting, as the weather was not suitable for flying the whole time. We were during this period the guests of various Norwegians, permanently living in Rome, and we received from them all the greatest kindness and friendly help. One evening we heard Riiser-Larsen give a lecture before the Geographical Society, but as he spoke in Italian we did not get much benefit from his lecture. The King was present, and after the lecture we were all presented to His Majesty, so even if the benefit from the evening, as far as the lecture was concerned, was meager, this last event made it a memorable time for us.

On the 26th Roald Amundsen and Lincoln Ellsworth arrived in Rome. That same morning all of us had been out on the flying-ground to be present at a visit from the King. His Majesty greeted us all kindly, then went through the ship, which had been hauled out on the ground, and later went for a short trial trip.

The day for taking over the airship now rapidly approached, and we were all looking forward to it with eagerness. She was really not yet ours, but when once that day was over then everything would be plain sailing, and, better still, a big step towards our departure from Rome also would be taken. Truth to tell, we would all be glad to get away from the partial inactivity to which we had been reduced.

Rumors also went about that on that day we should have the honor of being presented to Mussolini, a man with whom we should all be glad to have the opportunity of shaking hands. As a matter of fact, we had our first meeting with him, if I can call it so, on the Fascisti Seven Years' day. We had obtained tickets for the great festival which was being held on that occasion and there we heard him address about 100,000 people. We shall never forget the sight; he not only had the power of captivating his Italian hearers and followers, but us also, who did not understand a word of what he said.

On the 29th of March our beloved flag was hoisted on the airship, and immediately after this ceremony the ship was christened the *Norge*. From that time onward, unassailable recognition was given for all time to the fact that the ship and the expedition were Norwegian and none other.

Our desire to depart now rose to the heights. After the ceremony of taking over and christening the ship, we were presented to Mussolini, and for us all, I think, it was a moment we shall always remember. Later the Air Minister gave a luncheon, and that same evening Roald Amundsen and Lincoln Ellsworth traveled northward to join the *Norge* at Svalbard. One thing and another happily indicated that the day of our departure was rapidly approaching.

On the 31st Major Scott, the well-known English air-pilot, who was to be our pilot over England, came and at once won our hearts with his good humor and open, straightforward manner. A few days later the skillful French air-pilot Mercier arrived. All the various flying-grounds in France and England were now ready to receive us should we have need of them.

At first the crew were refused Easter leave because we were awaited at our destination. But a telegram from Rome was sent on the 31st of March which stated that the start would not take place before the 7th of April. It is hoped that the telegram procured the leave the crew desired.

The list of the crew and the apportioning of the work on board were settled at various meetings with Colonel Nobile. More Italians than was originally intended were included, but the plan was that these reserves were to leave the ship at Svalbard. At last on the evening of the 7th there came the long-expected message: "All men to be up to-morrow at 4.45 A.M. Departure from Ciampino at 10 A.M." Then was there bustle in the camp with packing and sorting without end.

We had instructions that we could take luggage up to 15 kilograms with us, but it is strange that when one begins to go through one's poor possessions on an occasion like this how difficult it is to pick and choose. In spite of the most honest endeavors, it was impossible to keep under the fatal 15 kilograms. We all had the 15-kilograms and perhaps slightly more when our baggage was weighed.

When we came out to the hangar there were not yet many people there, but at 9 o'clock they began to arrive, so that when Mussolini, with a large piece of sticking-plaster on his nose as the result of an attempt on his life the previous day, came soon after, there were quite a thousand people gathered there. The Norwegian colony turned up in full muster; we said good-by to them all and also to our other friends whom we had become acquainted with. Many were the hearty wishes we took away with us; and our friends the Italians on board the *Norge* received so many flowers that the ship looked like a flower-show. It was at first pleasant to have all those fresh flowers about us, but after they had faded we who were not the rightful owners were no longer interested in them and our fingers itched to throw them out overboard; but the owners were opposed to this!

It was, however, 10 o'clock and still there seemed little likelihood of a start; we strolled about and chatted with various people and—simply waited. At last at 10.30 word came that the start was postponed indefinitely, as the meteorological reports from France were not favorable.

We landed all our luggage again and went back to our boarding-house. Here our hosts, who were looking out of the windows and up at the blue sky, were suddenly astonished to catch sight of us all down below in the street—but their welcome was none the less hearty. None of them showed that they thought our manner of leaving Rome was at all strange.

In the afternoon of the same day we received a message from Colonel Nobile, through Riiser-Larsen, to the effect that our luggage was too heavy and that some bags and cases would be made for us at the factory. The next day saw us with some very small but very practical bags and cases made of rubber. They were so small that I think most people would even hesitate to take such light luggage for a week-end trip to the seaside. Yet with such small baggage we had to set off on a long journey of several weeks from Rome to Svalbard. Had a strong telescope been supplied for packing, accompanied by the following instructions: "First, using the glass the right way, look at the bag and the case; then turn the glass round and examine the things to be packed, and then fill the bag and case with them," we might perhaps have managed, but as things now were it was quite hopeless. Some of us solved the shirt problem very easily by purchasing Fascisti shirts, which, as is well known, are black. Thus the question of shirts for the journey was quickly settled. And the space in the bag had not yet been made use of. How splendidly we managed it! But, after all, I must say that even if we got over several such ticklish questions with such ease, the room for our things was still miserably small, as up north it was not really particularly warm at this time of the year, but we consoled ourselves that our flying kits, made of windproof material and lined with lamb's-wool had arrived. Thus clothed we should not freeze.

We discovered later, to our surprise, that the Italian crew were not supplied with luggage like ours at all, but on the contrary brought with them both portmanteaux and baggage of all shapes and sizes.

The meteorological reports from France were still unfavorable, but in Rome the weather was fine and calm. A fresh order, however, came in the evening: "Be ready for departure at 6.30 to-morrow morning." When we turned in that night we looked hopefully forward to the morrow.

The next day was the 10th of April and that day we shall long remember, for then at last we got away and the great venture began. We arrived at the hangar at 7.30 in the morning, and the first thing we set eyes on was a large, promising-looking case from Berlin, standing at the entrance to the pilot's gondola. "Thank heaven, there are our flying kits, so now we shall not freeze," were our first thoughts. There was a dress, helmet, and gloves made to measure for each Italian and Norwegian. For some reason or other, the case was unfortunately taken away right before our eyes and we saw it no more until we arrived at Svalbard. We went on board in the clothes we stood up in, and were not too pleased at the prospect of making the long trip to Svalbard in April, dressed only in ordinary sports suits. We were puzzled to know how the Italians would manage it, but we were, however, very soon enlightened.

Not so many people had collected as on the first time we were to start, but at least some hundreds had gathered, and they waved a last farewell to us when we started at 9 o'clock.

The weather was calm and bright when, after circling over Rome, we set our course for France. The first question that gripped our interest was whether we should succeed in reaching Pulham in one stage, or if the weather gods would compel us to land in France before we reached our destination. This fortunately did not occur. The intention, indeed, was that we should first fly across the whole of the Rhone valley through France, but unfavorable meteorological reports from there caused us instead to fly over to Bordeaux, and thence northwards.

At 6 o'clock in the afternoon we came in over the land after a splendid day over the Mediterranean—how wonderfully blue it really is can be best seen from the air. Now and then we took drift- and speed-observations, using as objects for this purpose small fishing-boats and some steamers we met with, whilst over the land we availed ourselves of houses and trees.

At 10 P.M. we passed over Bordeaux, which lay brightly illuminated below us—this was an uncommonly fine sight. It now commenced to blow and the wind increased little by little so that our speed at times was reduced to 40 kilometers. The work on board proceeded in its usual way; we who were told off to the rudders relieved each other there, whilst the other members of the crew were all at their posts.

There was very little sleep, partly on account of it being so cold and partly because the sleeping-places on the narrow keelson were, to put it mildly, Spartan-like. You can perhaps form a good picture of what these were like by taking three or four ordinary grooved washing-boards and laying them one after the other with the grooves upwards, then taking an ordinary life-belt, and rolling it together for a pillow. It is cold as you lie shivering on the washing-board with only a thin raincoat for covering. Such was the comfort the berths on the *Norge* had to offer us.

Let us, however, make a tour of inspection through the *Norge* whilst on her voyage to the north. We begin down in the pilot-gondola and there find the side-helmsman, who with eyes fixed on a steering-point either on land or in the clouds, keeps us to our course. Our steering-compass was, as a matter of fact, too slow to steer by. When the ship had been put on her course one took a steering-point ahead and kept her to that. This is indeed something that is common on all vessels and is well known to seamen. If the weather is still, she steers well, but if it blows and the weather is squally it may be a wearisome task to keep her both on her course and also at the right altitude.

On the starboard side we find the main-rudder

helmsman, who besides taking care that we constantly keep at the correct altitude (about 300 meters) has also to keep an eye on the gas-pressure gauges, and to see that the pressure in the various parts of the great balloon does not rise above the maximum allowed. In case this happens he must "draw gas." The wires from the gas-valves hang down in front of him, and it is then an easy matter to attend to these and by them reduce the pressure. He must likewise take care that the air-pressure in the balloonettes is correctly adjusted. This is regulated by means of a special little apparatus in front of the main-helm, which opens or closes for the air-current through the large ventilator in the bow.

On the port side we find Colonel Nobile, who keeps a watchful eye on all and everything. Just over his place are assembled the machine-telegraphs. The pilot-gondola was divided in such a way as to show that in front of here helmsmen and navigators were admitted. On the starboard side in front of the next section is the place for the navigators, who pass to and fro in the front part in order to give their orders to the man at the side-rudder when the course is to be altered. This part of the pilot-gondola contained the only two chairs on the *Norge*, which were constantly occupied by foreign journalists accompanying the ship. In the stern to starboard was our diminutive radio-cabinet, and between this and the gondola-partition on the port side was a small passage that led to the lavatory. From the front of this little room a vertical ladder leads up to the large open keel. If we begin our tour here right forward, where access to the top of the balloon also is, then we first come across the anchoring cables neatly hanging up, and the four girders. These cables are coiled up like cord, so that when they are let out through the holes in the side in the covering, which is stretched over the keel, they uncoil as they are released. Three of them are for the hauling down and mooring of the ship, and these are slipped direct from here on command from the pilot, whilst the fourth belongs to the cone at the point of the ship, and is used only for mooring to a mast. This one is released from the pilot-gondola and is hung up in a slip-apparatus that is worked from there.

We now go farther aft and pass the pilot-gondola, which lies quite open below us. Only the foremost part is covered with cloth and felt; the top of the radio cabinet is also covered with thin cloth. The keelson, which up to the moment has sloped downwards, is now nearly horizontal and does not begin to rise noticeably again until after we have passed the two foremost motor-gondolas. These lie right over each other about amidships, and access to them is obtained through two large oval holes in the cloth round the keel. From here we come out on to a narrow gangway with a slender rail in the front. If one is not accustomed to walking here one should hold fast to this rail. The gondola itself is suspended on wires whose dimensions to the unpracticed eye seem extremely slender, but there is no danger of their breaking as they are tested up to many times the strain they will be exposed to. In the motor-gondola itself there is little room, and if the motor is running and the radiator in the front open, there is a tremendous draught.

If we choose to go out on the starboard gondola, we find Omdal, smiling and placid as usual. This is his motor—the one, in fact, which never went wrong. The noise it makes is very disconcerting, making conversation difficult. In the pilot-gondola, on the other hand, people can talk together without any great difficulty. We leave Omdal, scramble back over the gangway stage, and draw a sigh of relief at finding ourselves back again in the ship.

On our way farther aft we observe the large petrol tanks which hang up on the frame-ribs on each side fore and aft. There are thirty-two altogether, the foremost and aftmost pairs are, however, used for water-ballast. On going to the motor-gondola astern we stop and peep down at our smiling Italian comrades—they are nice fellows all of them, good friends whom we valued highly. The keelson now begins to rise a good deal aft. Right after the cloth underneath is partly taken away, so from here we can observe the side-rudder. Our tour through the *Norge* everywhere reveals reserve parts, oil-tins, and tool-chests firmly fastened. A man hastens past us, disappears forward in the bow. Where in the world is he going? Up to the top of the ship to see that all the gas-valves are in order. Not a very attractive task. Through a small hatch in the bow one comes out on to the ship's nose and begins clambering, for on account of the bulge one has to pass it is hard climbing on the narrow ladder that is placed here. Care must be exercised over the first part of the journey, for here one passes over the thin cloth that is stretched over the steel-constructions which form the ship's bow; if one were to tread through here into the ship's interior, and if the speed and direction were good, one can be sure of falling through the thin cloth into the lower part and on out into space—with the prospect of making a not very pleasant acquaintance with mother earth 300 meters below! If this dangerous piece is passed one gets up to the top of the gas-balloon itself, and here one can stand up and walk along. Do not, however, try to be too clever the first time!

This walking tour is not so simple as it sounds, for to go across a full gas-bag, which yields under one, needs practice. After the first step one will find that the whole balloon goes along in waves, and if one does not do anything to stop the billowing, then at the next step one is pitched helplessly on to one's back, coming to rest hanging on to a line at the side of the balloon. This, of course, is not so very dangerous, as one can indeed haul oneself up again; it is not, however, pleasant. One should therefore take a course of training in walking up there. Having learnt the knack, the rest is extremely simple. One first takes an ordinary step, then immediately afterwards two short ones; thus is the wave-motion deadened and one walks just as securely as in one's own home. If one looks about one, however, perhaps a large majority would prefer their own home to the top of the *Norge*. As a rule, she is not absolutely steady, and one is reminded of a wild horse's tricky efforts to throw its rider.

She first puts her nose down, then one has the feeling of, "If I do not tumble off now, I'll be hanged if I ever do!" Just afterwards comes the contrary maneuver: upwards comes the nose, and, if one still hangs on, then she tries rolling to one side or the other a little. Add to this that she thunders on at a rate of quite 80 kilometers and is 300 meters above the earth, then perhaps you can form a slight picture of the work of the man who goes up constantly and sees that all is in order; but these fellows look equally happy and contented whether they are above or below.

On the trip to Svalbard it was the vivacious and happy reserve-rigger, Bellochi, who amongst other things also had this job; and from there the no less vivacious rigger Alesandrini took over this not very enviable task. These gas-valves of ours were quite big, being 12″ in diameter. When they have to be seen to one must always take care to secure them; this was the very first point that was impressed upon those who were given this work. Whilst the ship lay in the hangar at Ciampino, it happened that one of the Italian workmen forgot to take this important precaution; the result was inevitable—he simply lost the valve down in the gas-bag! There he stood with no reserve valve to hand and the gas streamed out in huge quantities. He was alone too, so could not send for help. If he went away the gas-bag would be empty before he returned, and that would be a bad lookout both for the ship, and perhaps not least for himself. What in the world should he do? Well, the fellow had presence of mind enough to place the plumpest part of his body over the hole, and there he sat shouting for help until some workmen down in the hangar heard him and came running to his aid with a new valve. If such a thing occurred during the flight, the result can be more easily imagined than described.

We rushed on towards France with two motors running. This gave us the most economic speed, namely 80 kilometers an hour with 1,000 revolutions of each motor. One beautiful landscape after another passed beneath us, and at 7 A.M. on the 11th of March we came out over the English Channel, near Caen. The night had been cool, so by now we shivered in our sports suits. How should we get on when we came farther north? The Italians were all supplied with fur-lined coats, so here was the explanation for their lack of interest in the flying-kits. Probably they really thought that the touch of cold we should meet with on the way would not trouble us, but the supposition was unfortunately incorrect.

The wind was still fresh from the east, so our speed was not great. Not before 3 P.M. did we arrive over the huge airship hangar at Pulham, where we did not land until 5 P.M. because of atmospheric disturbances. There were about 3,000 people collected to look at the *Norge*. The first we had the great honor to greet when we came into the hangar was His Royal Highness Crown Prince Olav.

We were all worn out after flying for approximately 32 hours, so we were glad to get to bed. Some of us were quartered with the Italians in barracks on the flying-ground, where we also ate our meals. The barracks themselves where we slept were pleasant—the only objection being that the partitioning walls between the different rooms were only built halfway. When at 5 A.M. one of the Italians began to talk to one of his fellow-countrymen in the diametrically opposite end of the barracks, it would be an exaggeration to say that Wisting, Malmgren, Omdal, Olonkin and I were particularly pleased; but it was no use protesting. They were real early birds and hailed the day with song and rejoicing! The old nautical saying that it is forbidden to smile on board in the morning before one has had one's coffee, was apparently unknown to them.

The very next morning we were at work again getting the ship ready for further flight. According to the original plan we should have lain at Pulham about a week, but this was given up, and the order now was that as soon as the meteorological reports were good and the *Norge* made ready, we should proceed. We were therefore very busy with gas-filling and preparations of all kinds. Our Spartan supply of provisions was supplemented at the stores of the station. During the flight we lived the whole time on preserved foods, chocolate, and biscuits; in addition each man had his thermos-flask, and when its contents were exhausted, we drank water. It was not possible to keep regular meal-times and every one ate when he had time. The food was not particularly choice, so when we came into "port" our first thoughts, reasonably enough, were concerned with getting something warm to eat.

Every one in Pulham was kind and pleasant towards us, and each did his best to make our stay as enjoyable as possible. In the hangar by the side of us lay the great English airship *R* 33. Its crew were our nearest neighbors in the barrack-town, and here we made many good friends. At Pulham we received an enthusiastic telegram from Roald Amundsen which gave us great pleasure.

Already on Tuesday the 13th we received orders for departure the same evening, as the weather was fine over the North Sea—indeed all the way to Leningrad. It came as a surprise to us, and our friends on the *R* 33 were disappointed that we should have to leave so soon. At 11 P.M. all was ready and a little after midnight we were again in the air and on our way towards Oslo.

It was quite stirring to see the interest with which the Englishmen regarded us. They perhaps looked upon the whole thing as sport, and as they do not betray their nature, their whole interest in ourselves and the expedition was at its highest. The farewell words sent after us by the chief "coxen" of *R* 33 when we started were characteristic: "Goodby, all of you, and a good trip. If any harm comes to you up there, we will take our old omnibus out and come up and fetch you." Yes, Englishmen are Englishmen all the world over—one of the most sympathetic nations to be found.

The ship was heavy when we started, so in the dark starlit night it almost seemed as if we only just cleared the tree-tops and roofs of houses that we passed. When we were well out over the North Sea, it became hazy, so that a man had to stand by one of the ventilators and cast a light down with a strong electric handlamp, in order that we might observe the reflection in the sea and so try to force the ship upwards in time. Fortunately all went well. The fog, however, took us out of our course, so that towards morning when there was a break we were over Denmark, a little south of Limfjord, and therefore the course was altered northwards towards Norway. The fog, however, set in again and forced us to rise over it. It was strikingly beautiful to fly over the thick fog, with blue sky and brilliant sun above us—it was like a rare and wonderful fairy scene. But quite another thing: the fog was not by any means pleasant for us, as it stopped our navigators from taking their drift observations. Now and then, there came great fog-banks rolling towards us, and then we could see nothing whatsoever. As we were afraid that we should, in the fog, collide with the mountains on the coast, we altered our course each time that those higher fog-banks rolled towards us.

A little before 9 A.M. the fog cleared and we then found ourselves off Arendal. We set our course towards the town. We circled over it and steered northward over Tromösund and along the coast to Aslo. In all the towns we passed, crowds of people were on the lookout and many flags were to be seen, but Oslo beat them all. This beautiful city beneath us reminded us of an ant-heap that we had disturbed with a stick. In the streets and on the house-tops and everywhere the people were waving to us. Those of us who had our homes here looked eagerly down. It is not at all easy to get one's bearing from the air, even if one is well acquainted with the land. But we found what we looked for!

At last, at 3 o'clock we were down and moored to the mast, and the preparations for proceeding were started at once. We hoped to get leave until the next morning and had counted on it, but the Meteorological Institute conjured up a little cyclone at some place or other over England which chased us away the same evening. It is scarcely necessary to add that our disappointment was keen. We were given about two hours in which to visit our homes, and therefore hurried off to find a motor-car we were sure the Reception Committee would have secured for us. Half an hour, however, was wasted before we succeeded in finding a conveyance.

I have often seen rows and rows of cars in Oslo, but I have never before seen the equal along the Ekeberg road on the evening of the 14th of April; my thoughts immediately flew to those days in Oslo when there was an international football match, but the rows of cars even then were nothing to what they were that evening. At last we arrived back to the flying-ground without any great trouble. Wisting however was not so fortunate. As a matter of fact, he was arrested. Some busy functionary who did not know him asked to see his ticket for the ground, and, as he had none, it looked like going badly with our good friend. A policeman, equally keen on his duty, hastened up and was about to lay hands on him when a civilian came to his rescue, and he was allowed to pass. But for all that, I think the whole of the district police force would not have succeeded in stopping Wisting that evening.

At 1.20 A.M. on the 15th they let go from the mast, and once more we were under way. It is impossible to guess how many people remained faithfully on the spot until the last moment, but there were many. When we started and heard the crowd sing, *"Ja, vi elsker,"* our National Anthem, rising through the dark night, we were all deeply moved. We then steered out over the fjord, and set our course eastward at Sarpsborg-Fredrikstad with Stockholm as our goal. The fog again came thick and close, and we had therefore nothing else to do but keep above it, whilst we hoped our drifting would not be too great—a hope that was unfortunately not realized. We had promised to fly over Stockholm and Helsingfors on our way to Leningrad, and so for this reason also we hoped the fog would clear; but, as I have said, we were unfortunately driven much out of our course, and we flew south of both cities; indeed, even if we had flown over them we should not have been able to see much.

At last, at 10 A.M. we sighted land. A more disconsolate-looking landscape it would be difficult to find—nothing but swamps, and here and there some clusters of trees with occasionally a lonely little farm. As we had not got any bearings by radio for some time, because it was impossible for us to get into communication with the Russian stations, our navigators were in doubt as to where we were. After some discussion it was agreed that we were over the northern part of Finland, and the course was accordingly set southward so as to find the Gulf of Bothnia, and from there proceed to Leningrad. But we flew on and on with no sign of the sea. The landscape changed its character a good deal, and we now flew over large stretches of forest and several lakes. But no sea. Several times we changed our course to the east, but equally without result. At 2 P.M., after we had followed the railway-line for some time, we found ourselves over a town, and here it was then decided to go down to a low altitude in order if possible to read the name of the railway-station. It was Varga. The map gave us the surprising information that this was a town on the frontier between Russia and Esthonia. So it was over South Finland we found ourselves that morning, and not, as we supposed, the northern part of that country. We were therefore not slow in steering northwards again with course set for Leningrad. Our thoughts during the whole tour turned not only to the land we left, but also to the land we were about to visit. We had indeed all heard so much of the Bolsheviks and their country that we were anxious to get the opportunity of judging their conditions for ourselves.

At 9.30 P.M. we landed at Gatchina in pitch darkness. It was therefore impossible to get a glimpse of our surroundings, but we could hear that there were many people about. The first we saw was a detachment of soldiers who stood ready to receive us. We looked curiously at their strange uniforms; it was chiefly their headdresses that attracted our attention, being something between a cap and a helmet. Otherwise they were dressed in long warm capes and large top-boots. This was necessary enough, for it was cold and the snow lay deep. My belief in the comradeship in the Red Army got its first shock here. Before the officer in charge began the maneuver of taking the ship into the hangar, he sharply gave his men to understand that he would stand no nonsense. There was no doubt about who was in command here. As I do not understand Russian, I ought to say that Olonkin, who as is well known is Russian born, stood by the side of me and translated everything. One thing we were particularly struck with here was that one man, and only one, had command, and thus the whole thing went smartly. In other words, the discipline was splendid.

One of our boys who had been on land with some telegrams came hastening back: "Here is something big, boys. There are a lot of horses outside waiting for us and we are going to stay at the Imperial Palace in Gatchina." That sounded very promising and we saw ourselves swaggering about in the former Imperial rooms. Lying on the long sledges which were strewn with straw, we then drove through the deep snow, and after having overturned several times we arrived, after three-quarters of an hour's ride to the palace, where we were welcomed in the library with a glass of steaming hot tea and sandwiches, which we appreciated very much, and to which we did justice. We regarded our hosts just as curiously as they regarded us, and there were many uncommon types amongst them. Afterwards, when we began to look about us a little and chatted about how pleasant it all looked, and wondered where we should sleep and so on, we were informed that these were not our quarters, and that this was merely a room reserved for Colonel Nobile. If we liked, however, to take our bags and come along, the distance was not very far. A moment later we went off, with a general as our guide.

We still looked brightly upon the situation—that is, the optimists; the pessimists, on the other hand, began to grow hostile. After a ten minutes' walk in the pitch dark we stopped at a house partially lighted up, but it did not look very inviting. Here we were received by an elderly woman, who conducted us through a dismal passage up an equally dismal staircase and into a hall, if I can call it so, on the first floor. Here we were to stay, if you please. We looked round, and thought woefully of the "Imperial Palace"—for this was truly something quite different from a palace. A large, square room, with four curtainless bay windows and about twenty iron bedsteads and one mattress, hard and uncomfortable, and one blanket and pillow, were all we saw. Not a picture on the walls; not a chair to sit upon. It was certainly not very grand, but we were tired out, and slept quite well the first night. But later it was worse. It is certain that the wretched sinner who had set our imagination working got his deserts now. The questions as to where we were and what sort of house this was occupied us considerably. The day revealed, however, a house quite pleasant to look upon from the outside. Let us, for argument's sake, call it a small palace! Then we set to work to solve the puzzle. The house or palace proved to have been built by the Tsar Paul the First in the park of his palace at Gatchina. He really used it as a kind of hunting lodge, but, as he was a man of simple tastes, he built it without any sort of luxury or accommodation. Bother the "simple tastes"; it certainly gave us shelter, but I

ABLE REPLY TO THE NORWEGIAN AERO CLUB, WHO WERE UNWILLING TO SPONSOR FLIGHT
EYOND THE NORTH POLE IN 1925.

should like to see Paul the First wash and dress himself in the tiny dressing-room we were given! I have never seen anything like it, even on an old sailing vessel. We were all installed here, Italians and Norwegians, so we had to make the best of very poor material, and I think we managed quite well, in spite of our long stay.

The day after, we were again in full swing out on the flying-ground, with the usual preparations for moving. As previously mentioned, the flying-ground was about three-quarters of an hour's drive from our "palace," so when, in the morning, we drove through the country town of Gatchina, or Trozk, as it is now called since the Revolution, we saw what it was like there. According to conditions, there was not much wrong.

The large airship hangar itself was built of wood. It had indeed gone a little to pieces, but was put in excellent repair for us. The only thing that was lacking was the large doors at one end, but as the hangar was much too large for the *Norge*, it did not matter. There was a strong military guard, and up in a house in the vicinity the officers and men had their guard-room and mess. Here we had a guard-room allotted to us, and we were very comfortable. The ground surrounding the hangar was protected with barbed wire, and guards were placed everywhere. We had printed passes issued to us, and had to present them every time we passed the barricade. The ship was certainly well guarded. When we came down from the guard-house we were first stopped at the porch by two guards. Out with the pass! A little farther on in the ground we were stopped by guard number two. Out with the pass again! This was again repeated when we entered the hangar, when guard number three inspected our passes. If we were in the hangar, and went out on the flying-ground to smoke, then we had to produce the everlasting pass if we wanted to go in again. It was no joke having these fellows about us either; for their rifles were loaded with cartridges, and, besides, there was one in the breech. I doubt whether the safety-catches were up either! The rifles were also superfluously armed with a long, four-edged bayonet, which probably could make a wound which would be very difficult to heal. If one came at night and wished to enter the hangar it was almost at the risk of one's life. Before one could say "Knife" there was an unpleasant-looking bayonet-point directed against one's stomach, and that, too, so unpleasantly near that one positively began to get strange feelings down one's spine. Out with the pass. . . . A short grunt, and then, with beating heart, one only had to go through the same trial a moment later. The most nervous of us, therefore, armed ourselves with a pocket-lamp, and with this in one hand and the pass in the other we went venturously along. When we approached a place where we supposed there was a guard, we had the pass out and turned the light on it. That was good enough when the guard was in the place he was expected to be in, but if he were not there, which was very often the case, the nervous were as badly off as the others—for then he popped up where he was least expected. I think it would have been absolutely impossible for an outsider to be able to approach the hangar either by day or night without being challenged. The guards were not posted at the doors only, but the whole ground around the hangar was full of them. As I have said, the guard was brilliant; they did not sleep at their posts—the discipline was too good and the risk too great.

At first we posted double guards there at night. On the second night Wisting and I had our turn. In the evening we were sitting in our nice warm room chatting when suddenly the door opened and in came four gentlemen. What now? Have we done anything wrong? Are we to be arrested? These were the first thoughts that haunted our minds. All the dreadful descriptions of Russia, of secret arrests, and an equally secret and terrible death, were the cause of these thought, I suppose. The gentlemen, who spoke perfect German, had quite a different errand, and a peaceful one. They came to enquire if we were comfortable, for, if not, then we had only to say so and everything would be arranged for our comfort. On the whole we got the impression that they, like all the military, were at our disposal. We had merely to express a wish and everything would be made as comfortable as possible for us. Truth to tell, we lacked nothing. It was like this everywhere; all were friendly and kind towards us; not once did we meet with ill-will. Everywhere there was a tremendous interest in the *Norge* and the expedition.

People came long distances to see the wonderful airship. Long queues stood outside the bounds. Here they were divided into parties of fifty, and were then taken round under the leadership of an officer, who explained the wonderful things they saw. It was no small thing to arrange, but never at any single point did anything go wrong. We could not help thinking of the crowds and queues we had seen in other places, where each had to push and look out for himself; there was nothing of that here. All went quietly. The first Sunday we lay there it was said that ten thousand people had passed through the hangar during that day. Cavalry detachments on splendid horses, and with their bands, came and went. In a moment they dismounted, and those of them who were told off to hold the horses did so, whilst the rest went through the hangar. We could not but admire the way in which it was all done. There was no shout of command to be heard; everything was quiet and orderly.

Some days after our arrival some engineers and

workmen arrived from Italy, and these now took guard over the ship, so from that time onward we had a real holiday. We made a trip to Leningrad, a visit we had all looked forward to, for now we should have ocular proof of the dreadful conditions that we heard prevailed in the old capital of Russia. But, so far as that was concerned, the visit was a sad disappointment. One is indeed apt to forget what the country has gone through, and one draws comparisons with one's own country. This is not right. If one takes everything into consideration, Leningrad is really quite pleasant. Quiet and order prevail everywhere; the streets are in good condition, and the houses look well kept. Several of the Russians with whom we talked thought that things were beginning to look brighter—an impression which we shared.

Here we also saw proof of the interest shown in our expedition, as the Scientific Association held a very well-attended meeting in our honor. Likewise the Geographical Faculty of the University gave a reception for us. There was a large gathering of enthusiastic people. Moreover, on the days we were there we went round the city freely and unmolested, and saw the lights. We saw the peerless collections of "The Hermitage," where schoolchildren passed round with their schoolmistresses, and had everything explained to them. We also went through the Winter Palace, where soldiers, under command of officers, were sight-seeing. At the opera one evening we had an unforgettable time: the fine ballet *Esmeralda* was performed. The house was very full, and great enthusiasm reigned.

On the 22nd word came from Vadsö that the mast was now ready, so it was only now necessary to await orders from Svalbard. On the 24th word arrived that the mast and hangar would not be ready until the 2nd of May. We were not particularly pleased at the prospect of a prolonged stay, as of course we all would be more than glad to get away and finish the first great stage of the flight. There were great discussions amongst us at that time. We also heard it asserted in some quarters that the flight before us was the most dangerous of the whole trip, even including that from Svalbard to Alaska. This was, of course, nonsense.

We tried, moreover, to shorten the time as much as possible. Most of us now stayed down at Gatchina at our "palace," but, other than an excursion to the village and outlying country in the vicinity, we could not find much to do to make the time pass. For the most part we kept to the "barracks"—I say barracks intentionally, for it was real barrack-life. Many jokes were made, causing much laughter, during these days. One was grateful for such entertainment. A description of how we spent our time is easily given:

On one wall hangs a paraffin lamp, yielding a

feeble light, just enabling those sitting under it to read! The whole of our library consisted of two books, which one of us, whom I will not name, had commandeered from Consul Platou in Leningrad. I hope our worthy consul will forgive the culprit when he hears what a joy those two books were to us. I do not think, however, that he would care to have them returned, for a well-worn public library book would look brand-new compared with the rags we left!

The time is only 8 P.M., but all of us are in bed, and then begins the chaffing. "Of course, you know that Swedes are awfully fond of anything to do with Royalty?" This comes from one bunk. Malmgren, who has been lying dozing, is wide awake at once. He needs to be awake, for there is no doubt in his mind that this time it is he who is the butt. The rest of us have no doubt either as to who is the victim, and Malmgren is at once the center of our interest for the next few minutes. A unanimous "Yes" from all of us sets the questioner going again. "Well, do you know what a real good north wind is called in Swedish, then?" Expectant silence, during which we all cast glances at the victim. "Well, it is called 'The Royal North-blast.'" The one who started the ragging gives the answer. There is general laughter. From that moment our good old meteorologist is called nothing else but "The Royal North-blast." Tobacco-smoke hangs in thick clouds in the room. In the other half of the barracks, which is only like a passage between the beds that separate us, the Italians are holding forth. Here also is much fun, but unfortunately we are debarred from sharing it, as in the case of most of us our knowledge of Italian is confined to shrugging our shoulders in the approved manner.

The weather at this time was changeable—from bright sunshine and calm weather to cold and rain, with a temperature down to 2° below zero, with snow. Our departure from here began to draw nearer. On the 29th of April we got word that, weather permitting, the start would take place on the 2nd of May. That day found us all out in the hangar at 2 o'clock. There were many people about. The weather was cloudy, with little puffs of wind from the north, which later freshened so much that the start was unfortunately postponed. It was just the same story here as when we started from Rome. This was Easter Sunday according to Russian reckoning, so we had the opportunity of celebrating Easter twice, as our Easter fell whilst we were in Rome. On this day we heard that the *Chantier,* with Byrd on board, had arrived at King's Bay, and that Wilkins had kept himself in readiness for the start at Point Barrow since the 23rd.

Not until the 5th of May did the weather permit us to make a start. We turned out at 4.30 A.M. and at 10 o'clock we were once again in the air and on our way northwards. The wind was northerly, and increased as the day went on, so our speed at first was not great, but fortunately later on it became better. We flew over Leningrad, and then got a good opportunity of seeing how large and beautiful the city is, as it lay beneath us, with its broad streets. From here we flew on over Lake Ladoga in a north-easterly direction until, at Lake Onega, we changed our course, and flew northwards along the Murman railway towards the White Sea. The wind was now very squally, and we were occasionally tossed about just like a ball. One moment we were driven high aloft by the gusts of wind, and the next we dropped equally quickly. It was a rough passage; still, there was not a single case of air-sickness the whole trip. The night was very cold, therefore sleep was entirely out of the question. It is true some of us had procured sheepskins in Leningrad, but they did not succeed in protecting us.

At 4 A.M. on the 6th we passed over Kirkeness, which lay sleeping beneath us. I do not know if it coincided with the time for general movement in the town, but all the factory-whistles sounded there as we passed. Perhaps it was, after all, a greeting for us, and a warning to the inhabitants to turn out if they wanted to see the *Norge*.

After circling over Vadsö, we moored at about 5.30 A.M. Despite the early hour the whole town was about, and flags were flying everywhere. Here we got a rare reception. The Chief Constable's wife, with a staff of kind ladies, had worked the whole night in order to prepare a festal welcome for us, and a most successful job they made of it, too. How many cups of boiling hot coffee were drunk I dare not guess, but that the coffee and the splendid breakfast—or shall we call it dinner?—soon vanished is certain. If one can judge of the success of a feast by the quantity consumed, then I think that none of our hosts at Vadsö had cause to complain! Afterwards we were invited to rest after the night; beds were prepared for us and were waiting (we could also get a bath), but none of us dared accept the offer, for fear that if we once lay down —tired as we were—our hosts would have great difficulty in waking us again for many hours. Besides, we were very busy.

The meteorological reports were favorable, and it was necessary to make use of the time, so already at 3 P.M. the *Norge* again sailed northwards. After having followed the coast for some time, the course was set for Björnöen. The weather was brilliant but rather cold. We hoped in the course of the night to be able to show the Italians our midnight sun, and in this we were fortunate. In the evening it was hazy, so our navigator was a little afraid that we should not get our bearings from Björnöen, as this, of course, would facilitate the navigation considerably. Had the weather been brilliantly clear we could have depended on seeing land the whole time from an altitude of 300 meters; that is to say, when we lost sight of the Norwegian coast we could expect to see Björnöen, and, in like manner, when Björnöen disappeared we could expect to see the South Cape rise up from the sea. But that did not happen, for when we had almost passed Björnöen we got a glimpse of it through the haze. The course was now set direct for the South Cape.

In the night the sun fulfilled our hopes, for it broke through the haze and made a beautiful scene. All our Italians were tremendously taken with the fine spectacle, but I do not think that they quite realized that the sun was shining in the middle of the night!

On towards the north the *Norge* flew. Now and then the sun forced its way through the haze, and now and then disappeared entirely from our sight. The speed was good the whole time. Then, at 2 A.M., we saw the South Cape appear out of the mist, brilliantly lighted up by the sun. It was fairyland. Snow-clad mountain top after snow-clad mountain top was fringed with the golden light of the sun. Such was our childhood's fairyland, in which white bears and princesses roamed side by side. We will visit that land. We went, and were not disappointed.

From the South Cape we hugged the land, for the weather was still changeable. We now had the opportunity of experiencing the snowing-up of the ship, which some of us had been very anxious about. Just before we came to the foreland we had a snow-squall. Not once did the snow get an opportunity of settling anywhere. If one looked through the windows of the gondola, the showers of snow lay horizontally in the air and disappeared astern. The throbbing of the motor, of which we had all become accustomed, towards morning almost died away. We began to look at each other. Had all three motors stopped? The port motor had indeed been damaged through running hot, so it was already out of action even before our departure from Vadsö. But that the other two should fail at the same time had not been contemplated. We listened anxiously. Yes, sure enough in the far distance we heard the sound of the aft motor, so something must be wrong with the starboard engine. It transpired that the cap in one cylinder had sprung, but we were promised that it would soon be in order again, and an hour later the motor was again running merrily. The danger of this motor stoppage was that we might be forced down on account of the greatly reduced speed, but fortunately this did not occur. The *Norge* held on, held on well. The repairing was a fine achievement on the part of our mechanics. The sections of the motor were so hot that there was no question of touching them. The one thing to do was to collect a lot of old rags together and carry the parts of the motor in them on to the keel, where the whole thing was repaired. Think of it! With the sea and ice 300 meters below them the boys went out on to the narrow gangway between the ship and the motor-gondola, with glowing hot sections of the motor, which were as heavy as lead. It was raw and cold too. We were partly prepared, however, to have to land on the ice. Our provisions were nothing wonderful, but with kind help in Russia we had been lent two guns, with ammunition, so that if we were driven to land in some place or other we might possibly maintain life by hunting. Close to the shore here we saw the first ice, and we got the opportunity of testing its solidity. When we trimmed the ship off the foreland ready for landing, we threw some sacks of sand-ballast overboard. These weighed about 20 kilograms, and, being thrown out from about 300 meters altitude, it was a heavy weight, but the ice withstood it. With excitement we followed a sack as it disappeared downwards with lightning speed. Would it go to pieces or not? This was the great question. Had we not been so dog tired I am sure that betting would have taken place with enthusiasm. Now it struck; and the sack lay in a thousand pieces. The huge weight, however, did not break the ice.

Ahead Cape Mintra appeared, and we rounded the point of the foreland and made towards King's Bay. The time was now still only 6 A.M. of the 7th, so the question arose as to whether our friends were quite ready to receive us. We looked forward with excitement. Where is the hangar? Yes, up there under the mountain stands a structure of remarkable appearance which must be it. Nearer and nearer we approach and below us we see Byrd's ship, the *Chantier,* and in by the quay lies the *Heimdal.* In between the ice floes under us two large white fish drift lazily along, and in on the shore we see one of Byrd's machines. Farther along, by the entrance of the pit, we see another; it is the huge Fokker machine, *Josephine Ford,* which later flew to the Pole and back. Soon we are above the landing-place, and there beneath us stand the landing-parties drawn up in the usual wedge-formation.

A little distance away is the mast, which has also been made ready to receive us, but fortunately we have no use for it to-day. The weather is perfectly calm, so that we can land right on the ground, and so get under cover as soon as possible. We are weary after having been on the go for about forty-four hours without sleep.

The landing-rope is cast out; all the men on the ground throw themselves upon it, and slowly we are hauled down. We begin to recognize our various friends, and soon the first greetings are exchanged. At 7 o'clock the *Norge* is safely brought into the hangar. The first 7,600 kilometers of the flight are over—but still the worst part has yet to come.

From Rome to Svalbard

The getting ready of the *Norge* for the final venture then began. Work proceeded day and night. The strangest rumors regarding the crew were circulated, but as time went on I learned that the hope of taking the supernumeraries would have to be abandoned. We had also the Italian reserve-riggers, Bellochi and Lippi, and they were just as eager as I was to go with the expedition.

In the afternoon of the 10th of May we received orders that the start would take place at 1 A.M. the next morning. Horgen and I, who shared a room, lay down in the evening and took it easy—he to rest ready for the efforts that were before him, I mostly for company's sake. At 11.15 the door opened, and in came Riiser-Larsen. "You must get ready," he said to me. "I cannot give you any hope, but there is still a small chance that you can come with us." Not a thing had I packed, so I had my work cut out. But still, it was only "perhaps." At 12 o'clock I was ready, and sat with my comrades at supper in the mess. Unfortunately, just after, a local wind blew which caused the start to be postponed, and so my chance disappeared into thin air.

At 7 A.M. of the 11th there was a stir in the whole camp, and at 8.30 all was ready. My hope of going with them was now very small. If we had got away at 1 A.M., then I think it probable I might have gone, but, now that the sun was comparatively high in the heavens, my chances diminished. The fact of the matter is that gas does not expand so much in the cold, consequently the balloon holds more, and is therefore capable of lifting heavier loads. If, on the other hand, it is warm, the gas expands, and so much must be drawn out again that the pressure is reduced to the maximum allowed. The sad news I received in the morning when I came up to the hangar was that they had already several times "drawn gas," and my hope sank if possible still more.

A little gust of wind now came, and the start was again delayed, but a little later it was still, and the *Norge* was brought out of the hangar. I left my own things alone whilst I helped with this work. After the *Norge* was out on the ground I went to say good-by to Colonel Nobile, but he waved me away. "Wait a little. Perhaps, perhaps." It was not pleasant, being tortured like this. I at once went back to the hangar to fetch my things, as I had to be ready at a moment's notice, should they have any use for me. Whilst I was returning with my knapsack on my back and the skis over my shoulder the *Norge* got under way. She steered northwards and disappeared.

My feelings? There was the *Norge* sailing away with all my comrades on board, friends I had learnt to know, and whom I valued. Now she bore them all steadily northwards towards the Unknown. It is not surprising that my disappointment was great.

"NORGE" OVER PULHAM, ENGLAND.

1. ARRIVAL AT SPITSBERGEN.

2. BYRD RETURNING FROM THE POLE.

From Rome to Svalbard

No wonder that I fought with my feelings as I stood there alone, left behind—lonely and forsaken as I had never been in my life before. But warm thoughts came, warm thoughts and wishes for their victory over ice, snow, and other difficulties. Thoughts and good wishes to the leader also filled me: the man who bore the whole responsibility, the man whose flight I had watched closely through the years, the man who, in spite of all difficulties, at last brought victory home—Roald Amundsen.

ROALD AMUNDSEN AND
LINCOLN ELLSWORTH

CHAPTER FIVE

Ready for the Start

CHAPTER V

When we asked Nobile when the *Norge* could be ready for further flight, he answered that if we wished it she could be ready in three days. A motor that had gone to pieces had to be exchanged for a new one, and gas and petrol had to be replenished. He also gave us to understand that the work might be hastened, and that he could do the whole thing in quite a short time if we wished to get off before Byrd. We explained to him the real facts of the case—that Byrd's object was the Pole only, whilst in our plans the Pole was merely a station on the way. We agreed then to make all necessary preparations quietly and steadily, so that nothing should suffer on account of hasty work. The tireless Höver-Zapffe combination was now omnipresent. It was necessary to get these weary and worn-out men to bed, and the work on the airship going as soon as possible. Major Vallini and Captain Precerutti went round amongst the many Italian workmen and superintended them with skill and zeal.

In the meantime the Americans worked with intense ardor. Several trial flights had been made, and in the evening of the 8th of May all was ready.

First Crossing of the Polar Sea

Taken all in all, Byrd and we are very similar. Thus we hate all farewell scenes; a warm and kindly "safe-return" is quite another thing. We also kept away from these last preparations for another reason, feeling anxious lest our presence might be regarded as intrusive curiosity. If, therefore, during those days we were not around Byrd from morning till night, the reason was simply a marked aversion from seeming obtrusiveness.

At 1.50 A.M. we were awakened from a sound sleep by the tremendous throbbing of a motor just outside our windows. In a flash we were out of our beds, and were just in time to catch a glimpse of the *Josephine Ford* as she got under way for the Pole. It may possibly interest those who constantly harp on this same refrain—"How disappointed you must have been that Byrd should have been the first!"— to know what passed between us at this moment. A firm, sincere handshake, with the words: "God grant all goes well with them."

It was a brilliant morning, just made for an enterprise of this nature. It was as calm as possible, and splendidly clear. Suddenly we both set up a shout of laughter; round the next corner came Berge, our photographer, sneaking along like a thief in the night. He had his camera and its tripod over his shoulder, and the well-satisfied smile on his face gave us to understand that he had trodden forbidden ground, with good results. Let us at once admit the truth: a more skillful and a more industrious man in his profession could not be found. Berge loves his work, with the result that he spares no efforts to "snap" what he wants. It is curious how a single occurrence will take hold of one, and always recur in one's mind whenever one thinks of a certain man. Berge was also our photographer last year at Svalbard. The incident we constantly talk of happened one bitterly cold April morning. The temperature was about 20° centigrade; it blew, and the snow drifted so that one could not see one's hand before one's face. We had just been out to a neighboring house, and were now running as fast as we could to get back to our own warm house as soon as possible. In our haste and in the drifting snow we nearly knocked a man over. It was Berge, with his ever-lasting camera. "What in the world are you going to do in this beastly weather?" was our very natural question. With a deep, quiet smile came the answer: "Photographing a snowstorm." We stood looking after him, for the storm and drift took him away out of sight at once. And that is the picture we always see of him—disappearing in the snowdrift. The thought, "One reaches one's goal with such people," naturally flashed through our minds.

The day passed as usual with preparations for our coming flight, but we found ourselves constantly stopping our work and looking at each other, saying: "How are they getting on now?" Byrd had chosen Bennett as his only companion, and, after what we had heard of this man, we knew the steering to be in most skillful hands. Navigating—that responsible and important work—Byrd did himself. But so extremely small a thing can cause failure in such a flight. Nobody knew this better than we who had taken part in the previous year's flight to 88° north latitude. We will attempt to analyze our feelings quite sincerely. The personal safety of Byrd and his companions, whom we had learnt to like as the excellent fellows they were, was certainly first in our thoughts. But—and there is a "but"—we often found ourselves remarking, "What will happen if they do not come back?" Obviously there was but one answer: We must look for them with the *Norge*. And then came the anxiety of having to upset our own great plans. There were, therefore, two reasons for our constantly recurring: "God grant that they come back safely."

At 5 P.M. we had all just sat down to our dinner when one of the Italian workmen rushed in, gesticulating and shouting: "I can hear a motor." We all sprang to our feet at once, and in an incredibly short time the mess was empty. It was true enough; there was no mistaking the sound of a motor, and soon afterwards we saw the Fokker, like a tiny black speck, high above the mountains to the north. It was an impressive sight; but there was no time to lose. It was necessary to be at the landing-place as soon as possible in order to give them the reception they deserved. It was rather a long distance to go, and not very easy to run in the deep snow. But we were really carried on the wings of excitement, and in a short time had reached the starting-track, along which we lined up at the place where the machine would have to land. In the meantime the aeroplane had come low down, and now hovered over the track for landing. This was not so easy, as the track was full of excited people running for all they were worth to meet the brave fellows. In spite of repeated signs from the fliers to clear the track, it was unsuccessful, and they had to make another circle before they could land. The landing was made in splendid style, and was so well calculated that the machine stopped exactly on the same spot that it had left in the morning. There were not many who had managed to arrive in time, but we were enough to seize and haul the two heroes out of the machine and to give them a rousing cheer. Then a strange thing occurred—we set upon the two men and actually gave them a kiss on each cheek! We were in a great state of excitement and allowed ourselves to be carried away by our emotions. Of all the compliments these two men have ever received, they have scarcely had a greater than they got from us at that moment. Nobody enquired, "Have you been to the Pole?" That went without saying, judging from the time they had been away. We knew exactly what these two wanted more than anything else in the world—namely, to get on board and into their bunks. Sixteen nerve-racking hours are enough for the strongest. So we asked no questions, but took them by the arm and led them down to the shore.

Despite the gravity of the moment, we could not help roaring with laughter, for, as we turned to go, what do you suppose met our eyes? Berge, right in the middle of the forbidden ground, working away with his camera with feverish zeal. But on such an occasion regulations were waived; anything was permissible. Berge obtained, as he afterwards told us, his greatest triumph here, as he was the only one who filmed Byrd's return. The photographers on the *Chantier* had not arrived in time. It is, however, highly probable that the photographers, whom Berge quite naturally rejoiced in having got the better of, had quietly photographed the whole scene from the deck of the *Chantier*.

Never were two cases of "medicine" more welcome than those we sent on board to that jolly crowd. We felt convinced that even the most bigoted teetotaller will admit that ice-water was not the right drink for such an occasion. The next day we dined on board the *Chantier,* and a solid foundation was there laid to a lasting friendship.

On the 10th we got word that all was ready for departure. It was then decided that, weather permitting, we should start as early as possible the next morning, in order to take advantage of the coldest part of the twenty-four hours. A local wind sprang up in the night, however, and prevented us from starting as early as we had intended. Not until later in the morning did the wind slacken, and the signal to "stand clear" was given. Getting ready to start was indeed an easy matter, for all had been instructed to bring as little as possible with them, so as to make room for the petrol supply. This was nothing new for those of us who had flown the year before, and, as the most natural thing in the world, we went down to the hangar with only what we stood up in. We did not even take an extra pair of socks with us. Still, we were properly clad. We had thick underwear, and all of us, with the exception of Ellsworth and Noble, were in good fur-lined clothes. These two were dressed in reindeer and bearskin clothes. In addition to the necessary rations for fifty days, each man took a small basket of eatables which consisted of sandwiches and hard-boiled eggs. Bert and Klara had been busy the whole night cutting sandwiches. They had also made coffee, and had filled about forty thermos-flasks. Last but not least, we had an enormous thermos-flask containing numberless quarts of bouillon with meat-balls. As, however, the bouillon in a short time tasted of the flask, there were only one or two of us, in the end, who enjoyed its contents. Horgen had double use and enjoyment of it, for he made use of the meat-balls and then used the holder as a seat. Meanwhile, it was so far into the morning before all was ready that the sun had begun to warm the top of the hangar, which was, as a matter of fact, without a roof. The result was that the gas expanded and had to be let out. At the same time a gentle local breeze made it difficult to bring the *Norge* out of the hangar. However, all came right again: the wind slackened, and at eight o'clock orders were given to bring the airship out. At the last moment we had to leave three men behind, so when the door at last was closed, we were sixteen men on board. Let us, before the *Norge* goes on her long voyage, stay a moment and see who these sixteen men were, and what position each one held.

ROALD AMUNDSEN AND
LINCOLN ELLSWORTH

CHAPTER SIX

The Members of the Expedition

CHAPTER VI

THE MEMBERS OF THE EXPEDITION

As leaders in this enterprise were Amundsen and Ellsworth. Many have said: "Yes, neither of these two is an expert in flying, and so cannot conduct a flying expedition." To this one can quite simply answer: "How often has it not happened that the leaders of a polar expedition have been inexpert in navigation and seamanship, and so have been obliged to appoint a skipper of the vessel?" Take such men as Nansen, Peary, the Duke of Abruzzi, Nordenskjöld, Mylius Erksen, and many others. None were seamen and therefore had to rely on assistance. But it is scarcely appropriate to say that they were incapable of sailing a ship and were accordingly unsuited to command expeditions. Herein lies the task of a leader or leaders—indeed, the greatest task: to select the best men for the various posts and to see that the whole machinery is in working order. If the combination is right, then all goes well. Of course, Nature may present such insurmountable obstacles that even the best-combined expedition fails. But the expedition that consists of unqualified men is doomed, be the commander ever so skillful. One man cannot carry out an expedition, but he can—with the assistance of qualified companions—conduct it to victory. We can in this respect say that the *Norge* expedition is a brilliant example.

As captain of the vessel we secured the best possible man to be procured—Colonel Umberto Nobile, the constructor and builder of the *Norge*. He had, moreover, ever since the airship existed, made a number of successful flights with it. The day we secured Nobile we congratulated ourselves, and all agreed that we had found the right man. On his appointment, Nobile threw himself heart and soul into the enterprise.

The next in command of the expedition and of the *Norge* was First-Lieutenant Hj. Riiser-Larsen, of the Norwegian Navy. He was entitled to this position as a matter of course after the flight of the previous year. It was he who also had the very important task of navigating the *Norge* from continent to continent—without doubt the most difficult piece of navigation a man has ever had to accomplish. He has also the qualification of being an airship expert. First-Lieutenant Emil Horgen, of the Norwegian Navy, was appointed to serve at the two rudders. He had taken part in the 1925 flight as reserve flier. He has many excellent qualities: A first-rate flier, quiet, self-contained, and calm, besides being a skillful navigator. Horgen has for a long time been employed as chief officer on the Nor-

The Members of the Expedition

wegian-American liner *Bergensfjord*. That steamship line was so obliging as to give him leave of absence so that he could take part in the *Norge* expedition. If Riiser-Larsen should require assistance in navigating the vessel, he had in him a most capable assistant. Horgen was given the side rudder. The main rudder fell to Amundsen's faithful and skillful old comrade of many years' standing—Chief Gunner in the Navy and captain of the *Maud* on her last expedition—Oscar Wisting. Captain Birger Gottwaldt, of the Norwegian Navy, was engaged as radio expert—the cleverest man in his branch. We expected much of him, and were not disappointed. On many occasions Gottwaldt, with his radio bearings, helped us out of awkward situations. Mr. Finn Malmgren, Graduate of Uppsala University, accompanied us as meteorologist. He took part in the *Maud* expedition from 1922 to 1925, and from it obtained enormous experience and practice in dealing with atmospheric conditions. In order to keep the world informed of the *Norge's* movements through the great unknown, the journalist Mr. Fredrik Ramm was appointed. Frithjof Storm-Johnsen was appointed at the last moment at Svalbard as radio telegraphist. It was with great regret we had to part with the member originally chosen for this post—the engineer and radio telegraphist of the *Maud* expedition, Genadii Olonkin. But this became necessary owing to an affection of the ear which he contracted. All these mentioned belonged to the large gondola, and would see each other during the whole flight—and perhaps more than they really cared about! The other part of the crew were quite separate from this one, viz., the part that looked after our three motors. We have therefore not previously mentioned Flying-Lieutenant Oscar Omdal, of the Norwegian Naval Air Force, as he belonged to the other part of the crew, and will thus be alluded to with the others who formed the motor-section. Omdal is made for such an enterprise as this. He was, therefore, the first member Amundsen applied to in 1922, when he began his research in the polar regions from the air. Omdal is the most agreeable, best tempered, and good-natured man one could meet. If we add to these qualities his remarkable skill in his own line, his resourcefulness, presence of mind, and willingness, then all will understand how invaluable he was to us.

The five Italian mechanics who accompanied us were selected by Nobile. They were chosen from the finest motor-mechanics in Italy. Chief-Mechanic Cecioni, Rigger Alesandrini, and Motor-Mechanics Arduino, Caratti, and Pomella—we were all very fond of these vivacious, good-humored sons of the South.

Then we come to ourselves. Is there any one who can be quite honest and sincere when he speaks of himself? But we shall try. Amundsen was himself quite clear that so long as he was in the air and all went well, his work would consist only in observing as accurately as possible the region crossed, and in describing it. There were specialists in every department, and there was no necessity at all for him to interfere with their operations. Moreover, he knew—and the knowledge was confirmed by the experience of a number of years—that he who has the chief leadership of an expedition, and accordingly the whole responsibility, ought preferably to be quite free, and prepared to come in anywhere if necessary. But—and whilst flying-technique is still in its infancy this is a very serious "but"—one must reckon upon being compelled to land, and, if the worst comes to the worst, to give up the flight. For such an event the leader of an enterprise of this kind must regard as a possibility, and must make his plans to face it. Here lay the greatest responsibility of all. All precautions were taken in case of a long stay on the ice, and the equipment was of the best possible. But, however careful and far-sighted one is, the unforeseen may occur, and then there is one resource only in such straits, viz., experience. What can a man who is inexperienced in work amongst ice and snow do in such a case? Nothing, absolutely nothing. He is doomed from the start. It would have been difficult even for experienced men, used to such conditions, to save their lives if obliged to go down far from land. But such men would always have a chance. Responsibility, therefore, rests heavily upon the leader, and this should not be forgotten in the rejoicings over a victorious flight. Ellsworth was on the go early and late, and helped wherever he thought he could be of use. Such a man does far more than he ever gets credit for. The specialist, who shows the result, gets the honor, whilst the man who lends him a hand is never mentioned. Ellsworth, smiling and contented, moved amongst them all, and took his share of the work in as equal a degree as any other man.

ROALD AMUNDSEN **AND**
LINCOLN ELLSWORTH

CHAPTER SEVEN

Across the Polar Sea

CHAPTER VII

ACROSS THE POLAR SEA

At 9.55 A.M. the order "Let go" was given, and
lightly and without effort the *Norge* rose grace-
fully up into the fresh clear air. It was about—4.5°
centigrade, and almost perfectly still. Our friends
below became smaller and smaller, and at last un-
recognizable.

Now that our connection with *terra firma* was
broken we were a little world to ourselves, swaying
lightly and freely in space. The motors were
started, and the *Norge* began the last part of its
voyage. It had been declared by some that the most
difficult part of the journey was over, but we wondered if these gentlemen were not a trifle uncertain
on this point. Who could tell what was before us?
Who dared prophesy?

Soon, however, we discovered we were not quite
alone, for Byrd's machine suddenly whizzed past us.
It was quite a comforting sight: there were still
other human beings in this world! The Fokker accompanied us for an hour and then turned back.

As has previously been mentioned, the gondola
was very small. In order to save weight the original
gondola had been cut down, and this had been done
so thoroughly that it was now extremely difficult

to find room for the ten men who were to be accommodated in it. When the foreign Press sought to give sensational particulars of the *Norge's* flight, and stated that discord and wrangling prevailed, that relations were even more like two armed camps, then there is only this to be said—that there was simply no room for quarreling. A certain amount of elbow-room is required for exhibitions of temper, but here there was none at all. Only under the most cordial conditions could this flight be accomplished, and we assure these imaginative gentlemen of the foreign Press that a more peaceful and tranquil spot than the *Norge* during the flight has never existed. Let it be said at once with emphasis that we never heard an angry word nor saw an unpleasant expression during the whole flight. And, indeed, how could anybody find time? That question seems enough to knock all ill-disposed fabrications to pieces. Let us take a glance inside and see how the situation shaped itself the whole time.

In the front of the gondola Horgen has settled down on his Bovril case. He is busy controlling the *Norge's* course, and has his time fully occupied. He dare not let go of the helm for a second. Well, then, Horgen is quite harmless. The next man we set eyes on is Wisting, at the main rudder. He is in the same class as Horgen, and entirely absorbed in a peaceful avocation. Amundsen is sitting on one of the two aluminum water-tanks, placed in the commander's cabin. He is for the most part occupied in the peaceful occupation of looking out through the window and studying the ice-conditions that are constantly changing. His gaze is often far away and dreamy: "I wonder what I shall see next."

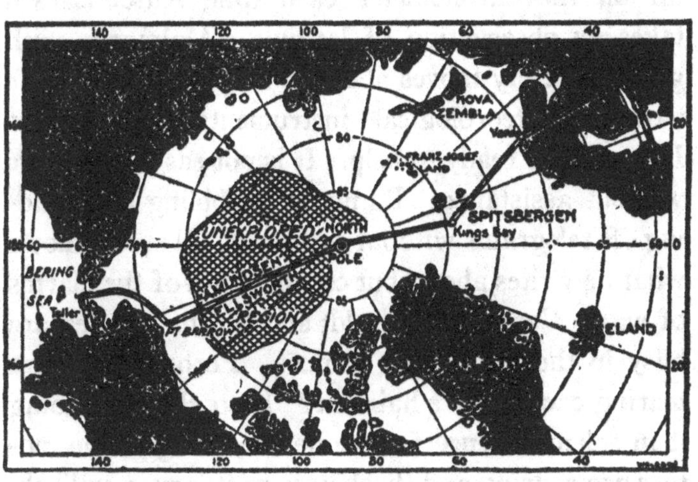

Everything around is unknown, and the most surprising object may show itself at any moment. "Land ahead" perhaps. How he can possibly get into a bloodthirsty frame of mind is difficult to imagine. Nobile is the fourth person in the commander's cabin. He moves about, smiling and composed. His movements consist in marking time, for no other space for exercise is available. Peace, then, prevails in this part of the ship. In the chart-room there prevails indescribable industry. The second-in-command is taking astronomical observations,

observations of drift and speed, which are constantly altering the position on the chart. This goes on incessantly and leaves no time for sleeping or eating or drinking, much less for quarreling. Ellsworth keeps calm and quiet, always ready to read off on the chronometer each time Riiser-Larsen takes an observation of latitude. Malmgren with great difficulty moves about in a circle amongst the various meteorological instruments. Here also Ellsworth is ready to help. It is not easy to manage without assistance. Ramm is scribbling and sending off telegrams without cessation. Heaven knows what he writes about, but certainly not of the alarms of war! Captain Gottwaldt and Storm-Johnsen are busy in the little radio cabinet. Perhaps they are tearing each other's hair out? If so, they are doing it in solemn silence for we hear nothing. The motors are roaring and throbbing, so it is very unlikely that the mechanics are looking after their work and at fisticuffs at the same time. No, dear scribblers, your "armed camp" was absurd and your stories untrue from beginning to end.

The feeling of safety on board the *Norge* was very much in evidence. Possibly this feeling was strong when we recalled last year's flight. In case any mishap befell the motors we could now merely stop and make repairs whilst we quietly floated on. It was very different last year. An accident to a motor was then synonymous with landing, and landing on this territory was in nine cases out of ten synonymous with a catastrophe. The ice-conditions seemed exactly the same now as in 1925. We did not see a single landing-place on the long way from Svalbard to Alaska. Not one. But it requires experience to be able to decide this. Several times some of our companions on board the *Norge* cried out excitedly: "See what a splendid landing-place." The four of us who had seen and experienced these "splendid landing-places" looked at each other and smiled—a smile that expressed our meaning better than any words. In spite of Byrd's fine flight our advice is: "Do not fly over these ice-fields before aeroplanes have become so perfect that one can be quite sure of not having to make a forced landing."

Flying northwards all went splendidly. If we did not look out and assure ourselves that we were in the air, we should not have realized it. The ice lay considerably farther towards the south than last year; it lay practically right down to Amsterdam Island. Whilst last year we saw broken ice right up to 82° N. latitude, this year we came in entirely over unbroken polar ice. But the humps were the same— always the same.

It is only under conditions like this one rightly comes to see what a remarkable age we live in. It is even stranger when we for instance are sitting in the smoking-saloon of one of the large Transatlantic liners and are enjoying our coffee with two or three friends, to get a little scrap of paper containing a greeting from dear ones, many hundred miles away. Still there are amongst us a few that are not so blasé that they do not on such an occasion exclaim: "It is very wonderful after all, this wireless." We elders, who have known nothing other than cables, will certainly never overcome this feeling. But we really first felt the complete effect when in 81° 30′ N. latitude. We received a telegram from a friend in Melbourne with his good wishes for our voyage. At 7 P.M. we stood with the headphones and listened to the time-signal from the Stavanger wireless-station. It was just as if we stood in our rooms at home and heard the clock ticking. It made a great impression on us. Here we were flying northward —always farther northward—into the great infinite ice desert, whilst at the same time we heard those at home sending us messages and trying to help us on our way. It is then that one can best realize what a wonderful age we live in. In 87° 30′ N. latitude Captain Gottwaldt was decorated with the King's gold service medal for his eminent work in connection with the radio. We had always admired His Majesty's great talent for doing everything at the right moment and in the right place, but this time we could not find expression for what we felt. With ringing cheers from us all, so that the *Norge* shook again, Captain Gottwaldt received the announcement of this high honor. That was the only time there was shouting on the *Norge!*

Across the Polar Sea

It is not easy to describe the feeling with which we now, lightly and safely, passed over our highest latitude of last year, 87° 43'. We do not know whether we shook our fists or not. Possibly we made a grimace and said: "Not this time, dear friend, not this time." It is most probable we took off our hats to our worthy opponent. Certain it is that we looked out on the humpy ice-field with endless relief knowing that we were over it and not on it.

As we neared the Pole the work of the navigator became more and more intense. He must endeavor to find the point as accurately as possible. We first had, however, another event to attend to—namely to celebrate Ellsworth's birthday. At 12 midnight all work ceased for a moment and all congratulated the esteemed leader who under such unique circumstances entered his forty-sixth year. This short ceremony, besides being a rare one, was also quite surprisingly pleasant, and Nobile conjured forth a flask of egg-punch. With handshakes and with egg-punch, therefore, we conducted the birthday hero into a new year. It will be long before he forgets it.

"Ready with the flags."

Riiser-Larsen knelt and through the open window followed the sun with his sextant.

"Now we are there."

Out flew the beautiful double-sewn silk Norwegian flag. It was on a cross-bar fastened to a long aluminum staff exactly like a standard, which resulted in its making a splendid descent. It landed correctly, fixed itself in the ice, and the light breeze unfolded the Norwegian colors. Amundsen at the same moment turned round and grasped Wisting's hand. No word was uttered; it was unnecessary, for these two men's hands planted the Norwegian flag at the South Pole on the 14th of December, 1911.

Then the Stars and Stripes flew out. It was with an extraordinary, quite indescribable feeling that Ellsworth undertook this task. When again will a man plant the flag of his country at the Pole on his birthday? Not for many a year perhaps. Lastly Nobile threw down the Italian flag. Thus all three flags stand a few yards apart as near the Geographical North Pole as any human beings can determine with instruments. It was then 1.25 Greenwich time on the 12th of May, 1926. Ellsworth received two congratulatory telegrams here from relations and friends. The ice was much broken up at the Pole and a mass of small ice-floes was observable. It was quite different from the other ice we had passed over. We were uncommonly fortunate with the weather, having as a matter of fact, been in fog just before reaching the Pole. This disappeared, however, and permitted our navigator to take his observations.

As the technical sections of the book will probably contain a mass of figures, such as the time of day, temperature, distances, speed and so on, we shall endeavor as far as possible to avoid them in this our part.

The ice continued in a very broken-up condition, except with a few closer-packed stretches right down to 86° N. latitude. There it assumed quite the same character as the ice between Svalbard and the Pole, and at the Ice-pole itself there was not a particle of open water to be seen. The Ice-pole—or, as it up to this time was called, the Inaccessible Pole—is the center of the great ice-covered region and as such, of course, is the most difficult place to reach.

Of animal life we had seen extremely little. North of Svalbard we saw a good many bear tracks and indeed two bears. They were so alarmed when they saw and heard us that they threw themselves head-first into the nearest opening in the ice. We saw no more bear tracks until we came to the Ice-pole. There were no signs of bird life, nor of seal nor walrus. This was only a confirmation of the previous year's observations.

At 8.30 A.M. we came into a thick fog and this kept on with occasional breaks until 6 P.M. It was thus a tremendous sea of fog we passed over and in some places of extraordinary density. It is clear that this, in a high degree, prevented our taking observations. We may well therefore have passed over islands at low altitude. There can be no question that land exists, even flat land, to any great extent on the course we took, as we time and again observed the ice under us. The greatest danger we encountered on our journey was met here. The damp fog settled in the form of ice on the various external metal parts. This ice became loosened from time to time, was sucked into the propellers and was then slung against the outer part of the balloon-envelope, with the result that it was much battered and had constantly to be repaired.

At 6.45 A.M. (Greenwich) on the 13th we sighted land on the port bow. It was a great moment. The flight had been accomplished and the goal reached! It is difficult to obtain land-bearings in these parts of the world and especially from the air. The flat land seemed all alike—a heap of gravel here and there. Wherever we were on the Alaska coast we had to alter our course westward along the shore so as to come out in Bering Strait. We supposed, however, according to the last observation, that we had struck the coast some miles west of Point Barrow, but we did not see it. That our supposition was correct was proved a little later, as we then passed over Wainwright, Amundsen's and Omdal's place of sojourn from 1922 to 1923. We were now no longer in doubt. We knew every single house. The inhabitants had heard the sound of the motors, and all of them had collected outside on the slope. What in the world were their thoughts? They expected indeed that we should come, but it is scarcely reasonable to suppose that they had formed any concep-

1. KING'S BAY—HAULING MATERIAL FOR THE MOORING-MAST.

2. THE HYDROGEN TANKS.

THE HANGAR AT KING'S BAY.

tion of the real appearance of an airship in mid-air. Indeed, to us an airship seems an imposing sight. What then must these people think when such a monster suddenly shoots out of the clouds? Some years ago they would certainly have shot at us. Not so now; they knew that Amundsen and Omdal, their good friends, were on board. All waved and shouted and took their hats off. But it lasted only a moment before Wainwright was lost to sight. Shortly after we passed over our own familiar Maudheim, the house we ourselves had built and had lived in for a whole year. The people who now lived there all gathered on the roof and clearly showed their excitement. Memories came and went. On the 20th of November, 1922, Amundsen left this house with one Esquimau, one sledge, and fifteen dogs in order to go southward to more civilized regions, whilst Omdal remained behind to look after the house and the aeroplane. They accomplished the journey to Kotzebue Sound in ten days—a distance of 500 miles. It was a fine achievement for a man who had passed his fiftieth birthday—fifty miles a day for ten days. There was no question of sitting on the heavily laden sledge; not the slightest. They walked the whole way, holding on to the sledge for support. It was a record trip of high rank. But now we could record something considerably greater. Soon the house had disappeared and the journey began along the low coast covered with lagoons. It is difficult enough to proceed with sledges and dogs in this kind of region, as the land often entirely disappears. But from the air it is still worse. At Cape Lisburne we came into a fog, so we rose and sailed above it. We were obliged to be at a considerable height so as to be sure of clearing the mountains. Our journey from now onwards—after the real voyage was ended—became the most adventurous. A furious gale blew up from the north, and partly in and partly out of the fog we drove quite out of our course. Probably we were, according to observations, at about 6 P.M. (Greenwich) on the 13th of May, not far from Cape Serdze Kamen on the Siberian coast. We then set our course due east so as to reach the coast of Alaska again. At 11 P.M. (Greenwich) we at last reached the coast. An observation showed us to be in the vicinity of Kevalina on the north side of Kotzebue Sound. Here we had quite a pleasant experience: we saw a hut with an Esquimau and his dogs outside it. We passed in over the land at quite a low height above him. He danced and gesticulated. What his thoughts were we leave the reader to imagine.

Ice conditions in the Polar Sea, north of Bering Strait, were peculiar. Here—where we year after year had tried to force our way northwards, drifting with the *Maud,* but had met with quite impenetrable ice only—it was now quite open. Indeed it was so open that we thought that we had been driven out into Bering Strait before we got our bearings. From Kevalina it then bore southward along the land. We also got our bearings from the Serpentine River, which from the air is impossible to mistake, with its distinct snake-like twists. Here we had another experience, as, at quite low altitude, we passed two Esquimaux with their dog-teams. We were then so low that we could very easily have recognized them had we known them before. The dogs were, as can reasonably be imagined, startled, and we can well suppose that their owners were also, for they had difficulty in managing them. The journey from here along the coast was not altogether pleasant; the northerly gale had increased to a storm and the drifting of the immense balloon became considerable. At times it appeared as if it would be difficult to prevent it from drifting in over the high mountains on Seward Peninsula. All went well, however, and we passed Cape Prince of Wales at 3.30 A.M. (Greenwich) on the 14th of May. Bering Strait was quite free of ice, and the strong wind over the open sea was very troublesome. We could now really feel the difference between a flight over ice and one over sea. We had during the long voyage over ice been accustomed to absolutely calm conditions. It was now quite different: like a ball were we tossed up and down by the strong wind and not infrequently the *Norge* drove sideways through

Bering Strait. In order to have all in readiness for landing, which should now, according to our plan, soon take place, Riiser-Larsen wrote a note to the acting Norwegian consul, Mr. Ralph Lomen, with detailed instructions as to what was to be done from the slope during landing. The coast, however, had entirely disappeared in the fog. The wind howled worse than ever and the apprehension of drifting out of our course and out into Bering Strait was not groundless. In order not to be exposed to this the airship was steered towards land. We were now in "waters" with which both Amundsen and Wisting were familiar, after their various trips in the course of years. As Wisting was fully occupied at the main-rudder, it fell to Amundsen to act as guide. There is an enormous difference between acting in this capacity on sea and in the air. One is accustomed to the former; but the latter one is totally unfamiliar with. When you add storm and fog to this, the "guide's" position is not an enviable one. As we steered towards the coast we saw faint outlines of an island on the starboard side. In the haste and tumult that now arose in making all ready for landing, Amundsen took this to be Sledge Island and we hugged the coast expecting that before very long we should be at our destination. Under more tranquil circumstances one would scarcely have committed such an error as this, but conditions were far from tranquil. As mentioned before, there prevailed chaotic disturbance—everything having been brought down into the lowest gondola in readiness for anchoring. It if had been crowded before, one was now entirely prevented from making the slightest movement. That part of the coast we now came to appeared quite strange, a fact (as was later proved) that was not so very remarkable, as we had never been there before. At 7 A.M. (Greenwich) on the 14th of May we reached a spot where there were a few houses. What could this be? Not the originally intended landing-place, for the houses were too few, and moreover were lacking that best of identification marks, the high telegraph-mast. We now all agreed that a landing ought to be attempted, especially as the ice was even and unbroken outside the little village. We would not, however, give up finding the landing-place originally fixed upon without first examining the coast a little. This was then done, but without result. The "guides" had to acknowledge that they had never been here before. Now came the question, Should we leave the place where conditions seemed—though this is not saying very much—better than any other place? Besides we got the announcement that we had petrol for only seven more hours' flight. We believe, we venture to say with conviction, that all on board desired to land even if it were risky. It must be remembered that we had been in the air for about seventy hours, and most of us entirely without sleep.

The result was that we were dead tired and unfit for work. Indeed, some even began to see visions. During our flight to and fro we again came to the little village, which now with its small, even surface of ice gave greater possibilities for a safe landing than any we had hitherto seen. The wind here was also strong and came in dangerous squalls, but there was some protection. "All right, then let us try." The landing was one of the achievements one will always remember. It was splendidly done and we take off our hats to the skipper of the vessel for the quiet, neat manner in which he accomplished it. But if conditions had remained the same on landing as when we started, the result might well have been doubtful, even if the skipper had been ever so skillful. But the remarkable thing happened—it can well be called the miracle—something that causes us to sometimes stop and think. There must indeed be an over-ruling Providence. Whilst we were descending there were still strong, quick gusts of wind from the land. Suddenly, and without any warning whatsoever, it became quite calm and remained so during the time we were landing. As we began to approach the ice, people came running out to meet us. An attempt to anchor the airship failed. The ice was too poor and the anchor that was cast out could not grip. Nor was it really necessary. Gently and quietly we approached the ice—nearer and nearer until we at last touched. The gondola was supplied with an enormous air-fender on the bottom, so this overcame the shock. But for the bump against the air-fender causing us to spring some meters into the air, we should scarcely have noticed the landing, so finely and skillfully was it done. The ice we landed upon lay just outside the village. The whole population had now come to the spot and most of them helped to hold the anchor-rope. The door of the gondola was now opened, and one by one we jumped down upon the ice. They were a peculiar people that we found here: they did not show the slightest perturbation or excitement; quietly and calmly they gave us a warm welcome. One would almost think that they were accustomed to receive airships every day. At last we got our curiosity satisfied: "Where in the world are we?" "In Teller," was the reply. We had therefore flown ninety kilometers away from our original landing-place.

The first flight from continent to continent via the North Pole had been accomplished without any injury whatsoever to any one.

Honor be to whom honor is due. Let us then be of one mind in giving to Him the honor Who on several occasions on this venture clearly and distinctly held His hand over us and protected us. Let there be no dispute as to who amongst us was the best. We are all so pitifully small, if God the Almighty does not help us.

CHAPTER VIII

Alaska, Alaska, land of adventure! You tempting, inviting, soul-stirring land. How many have you tempted with your gleaming gold? How many have you brought to the dark abyss of despair? There are few who have left you again with the smile of victory on their lips; it is said that every dollar that has been taken away has cost two. These and many other thoughts passed through our minds when we left the boat that brought us from Teller to Seattle.

It was here Amundsen landed in the autumn of 1906 after having accomplished the North-West passage, welcomed by many thousands of people with music and shouts of triumph. It was here the crowd in wild excitement raised him on their shoulders and carried him through the streets of the little town to the place where he should stay as the town's guest. What a night! It seemed as if the champagne of all the world, stored up for many years, was set flowing. Big and little, old and young, all indeed took part. And why not? It needed only to bend down and grasp the soil and rise again with hands full of gold. The production of gold seemed inexhaustible. This peaceful, quiet little beach, where a few years before only Esquimaux and now and then a whale-fisher came, was now a small modern town. The anchorage lay full of steamers that waited to discharge their cargoes to the impatiently waiting people, in order to go back again with gold and with joyful men. And the people themselves? There were all kinds of them, both good and bad, but the typical pioneer was, however, the most prominent—the serious, honorable, hospitable, and hard-working man. Full of good humor he was, and full of an unconquerable faith in the future. It was this type of man that set his mark on Alaska in those good old days. One felt good to be with them; made one long for them when one left them, and made one never feel satisfied until one saw them once more. The air, the people, the conditions—indeed everything—seemed to have sown a seed in one's heart that developed little by little, and at last drove one back to its native soil there to spring forth and unfold.

In a bewildering confusion these pictures of those great days flashed through the mind, when on that May morning we again set foot on the aspired ground. The flight, which had quickly brought these people into communication with the other side of the globe in a few hours, might well represent for them something great and uplifting. Let us then admit it at once. We expected this time also to see the happy crowds come jubilantly to meet us. But we were mistaken. With the exception of our very best friends, five or six of them, who smilingly bade us welcome, the place seemed deserted. It was a beautiful morning. The sun shone from the high heavens—cloudless sky and nature herself appeared to have put all in order for this memorable arrival. It was early in the morning we must admit, but the clock plays no part in summer in these regions. Day and night are alike. The streets, which we remembered as full of people, lay still and deserted; the houses looked crumbling and bare; and the pavements, once so well-kept, lay in a heap of ruins as if the result of a violent bombardment. We must certainly have allowed our astonishment at this changed condition to appear in our faces, for one of our friends drew us gently to one side and anxiously and hesitatingly said: "Look here, we had expected the airship to come here now, but as it did not the people are a little disappointed. We really made many great preparations and now they are all in vain."

So this was the reason for this cool, inhospitable reception, because, to save our lives, we had gone down some few miles away from this place that we had hoped to reach. Then we understood that the old hospitable race of pioneers we had known in former days had been replaced by modern, cold-hearted, money-grubbing individuals who had nothing in common with the great, beautiful land of adventure—Alaska. We spent about four weeks at this place and, if a friendly thought goes back there, it is due entirely to a small handful of faithful friends, the only ones surviving of the old pioneers. On the 12th of June the *Victoria* came north from Seattle and brought new life with it. It was with glad appreciation that we saw these people set foot on that ground and rouse the benumbed inhabitants from their winter slumber. How interesting it was to see the difference between the permanent resident and the newcomers! From our own experience we know indeed how that secluded life seizes upon the sound, reasonable capacity of thought. One year leaves its mark on an individual. What then of those who live so cut-off, year after year? Without their having any suspicion of it themselves, their brains contract to a minimum and we can then indeed imagine what is the result, when these persons so mentally affected begin to judge with that little bit of brain that is still left them, as if it were still in full vigor. The contact with the newcomers helps remarkably at the beginning and the most interesting changes can be detected. But then very soon comes the winter again and the isolation begins anew. Then the mind is quickly attacked and it is not a few individuals who year by year go from Alaska to recruit the asylums in the States.

On the 16th of June the *Victoria* again steered

southwards, and we must admit it was with a sigh of relief that we saw the land disappear beneath the horizon. The voyage south was extremely pleasant and, with the exception of two or three short stays at the Aleutian Islands, we went direct to Seattle by the shortest way. What was to await us? Would they also treat us coldly because we had not endeavored to fly there?

Conditions on board the boats in these waters are quite peculiar. The democratic spirit has attained a higher development here than in any other place we have journeyed to.

Thus passengers and stewards associated like good comrades. Class-distinction is quite obliterated. On one of my previous voyages on the same boat it chanced that at the close of the journey one of the passengers gave his table-steward a smaller tip than the latter deemed adequate. What happened? Well, the steward invited the passenger on deck in order to give him a proper drubbing. But, alas, our good steward had reckoned without his host, and the matter ended in the steward getting the sound drubbing!

On the first voyage north and the last one south there is usually immense activity: every inch on board is occupied and not a single bunk is to be found vacant. That the passengers do not belong to the ordinary traveling class is apparent from one of the notices to be found fixed up on the wall of each cabin. It reads something like this: "Passengers are requested to take off their boots before going to bed." And also: "Gambling is most strictly forbidden." Well now, that is a very good regulation. But, when you find in every cabin a folding gambling-table for general use, this does not help in the observance of the regulations.

The *Victoria* is a very old boat, but built at a time when the best materials could be made use of, so she is still solid and strong. She has undergone numerous alterations in the course of time, and has developed into a modern passenger-boat. Thus she has six first-rate modern cabins complete with bath. The *Vic*, as she is generally called, is everybody's favorite, and really deserves to be so. The captain, Davies, and his officers are all old and experienced hands in these waters and deserve the full confidence of every one.

On the 27th of June we came down into Puget Sound, that wonderfully beautiful arm of the sea that leads into Seattle, Washington. Having passed Port Townsend we should no longer be kept in doubt as to the attitude of the American people towards our flight. Deputations from the Chamber of Commerce and other public institutions met us here and laid before us the many and great preparations that had been made for our arrival. Shortly afterwards one aeroplane after another whizzed over the old *Vic* and gave us clearly to understand that here the

1. ARRIVAL OF THE "NORGE" AT KING'S BAY.

2. SHOWING THE 250 H.P. MAYBACH MOTORS.

READY FOR THE FLIGHT.

Ellsworth wearing the polar bear pants worn by Byrd on his flight.

cold had vanished. It was an unforgettable moment when we lay to at the Alaska Steamship Company pier at Seattle. Huge crowds were collected to welcome us. We must have presented a strange spectacle as we stood by the ship's side and received the first greeting of the American people. Most of us had nothing other than what we had procured in Alaska—the ordinary gold-digging outfit. Indeed, we had been warned that owing to the great weight nothing could be brought with us, and we had of course kept this order. It had therefore a surprising as well as depressing effect to see Colonel Nobile and two of his Italian companions in gorgeous uniforms. Resentment filled us when we saw this, but of what use was it to be angry? The flight was over so now it was neither here nor there. We were not quite sure that we should have mastered our feelings so well if we, for some reason or other, had been compelled to go down on the ice and walk home. It is quite possible we should have had something to say about military uniforms on polar expeditions.

The reception in Seattle was marked by enthusiastic warmth and hospitality. The Mayoress of the town, Mrs. Landes, was the first to bid us welcome; then representatives of the Governor, the Army, and the Navy. We were driven in a number of luxurious motor-cars to our hotel and installed there with the best accommodation. The next day the town of Seattle gave a banquet for us, and on the same evening we went eastward with New York as our destination. We had to reach there on the 3rd of July, the *Bergensfjord's* departure being fixed for that day. We could do it, but only just. Our journey through the States will remain as a bright recollection for us all. There had been great competition between the various railway companies as to which of them should convey us across. We chose the Great Northern's Oriental Express, as we had been told it was the most luxurious and comfortable train between the two coasts. It will bring a smile to hear that we, who came from the humblest of what the world can presumably offer in the way of comfort, now looked round in all directions and carefully sought to make sure of getting nothing inferior to the very best of what American luxury and accommodation could supply. We fully succeeded in this, the company having placed a private railway-car with bedrooms and drawing-room at our disposal and also our own dining-room. The three days and nights it thus took us to reach Chicago were therefore a dream of well-being. The company sent its own representative, Mr. Meldrum, with us in order to make sure that we lacked nothing. Our mode of living was now suddenly changed from that of a vagabond to that of a prince. We got up when we wished, lay down when we wished, and enjoyed the most delicate meals. We could not help thinking of the play, *Jeppe paa Bjerget*. We pinched ourselves when we pressed the button in the morning and ordered the smiling negro attendant to put our bath ready. We studied his face most carefully when he, coming in with a broad grin, answered: "Yes, sir, at once, sir." What if he were fooling us? We pinched ourselves again when he disappeared through the door. It hurt, so it must be ourselves right enough! We were not, however, quite certain until we took the refreshing morning tub whilst the train whirled along at a speed of over sixty miles an hour.

The journey seemed like one single triumphant procession. Telegram after telegram streamed in with requests for us to show ourselves on the platform of the carriage in order to receive the homage all seemed to desire to offer us. Thus everywhere we were met with the warmest and most intense enthusiasm, and very delightful it was to note that it was the American nation that came to greet us, and not our own fellow-countrymen alone. We have the conviction that the cool attitude of the north towards us urged these good-hearted folk to put double fervor into their feelings, so as to show us that they valued our work more highly. It can be readily understood that we felt an extra strong thrill when we passed through the thickly populated Norwegian districts. Which of us will thus forget Ninot in North Dakota? There was an exhibition just being held there and we were requested by telegram to come out on the exhibition ground for half an hour. We accepted the invitation after having been assured by Mr. Meldrum that the train would not leave us behind.

On arrival at Ninot we were at once ushered into the waiting motor-cars, and at a furious speed were driven to the exhibition, which was being held a quarter of an hour's drive outside the town. It was an imposing and affecting sight that greeted us on our appearance. There were about twenty-five thousand people present. It was a brilliantly clear day with just enough breeze to unfold the hundreds of American and Norwegian flags. These masses of people had taken their places on two giant grandstands. In two lines, leading from these to one opposite, where we were to be placed, stood the athletes of the town, holding the Norwegian and American flags alternately. Thousands of Norwegian flags were waved from the grandstands. Just as we ascended the little platform intended for us, with its front directly facing the mass of spectators, there burst out to greet us the tune of the Norwegian National Anthem, *"Ja, vi elsker dette landet,"* played by an enormous military orchestra. We stood a moment as if rooted to the spot. This came so unexpectedly. Time after time came the feeling, the strangely peculiar feeling, of a lump in the throat. You swallow and swallow, but there is nothing to swallow. It was a real struggle to keep back the tears. We shall never forget Ninot. The railway-line ran just past the exhibition-grounds and we had the thrilling experience of seeing the Continental Express stop right out in the open country to pick us up. Such a thing does not occur every day—perhaps never again. The salute boomed out and Ninot disappeared, but took its place amongst the many beautiful memories.

It is difficult to say how many thousands were collected at the station at Fargo, in North Dakota. There must certainly have been several thousands. The train was suddenly surrounded, and it had difficulty in coming away again. At the urgent request from St. Paul and Minneapolis we decided to pay the twin cities a visit. They stand like two powerful rivals on the banks of the Mississippi. We will not risk any opinion at all as to which of these two has reached farthest on the path of development, but one judgment we can pass without a quiver, and that is that in warmth of hospitality the twins stood on one and the same level, as high as they can possibly come. We spent some pleasant morning hours in the home of our kind consul, Mr. Hobbes, where we had an excellent breakfast. Later we were the guests of St. Paul for luncheon and the guests of Minneapolis for dinner. Our two railway-carriages were at this time uncoupled from the train in which we left Seattle, and were in the evening coupled on to the next outgoing train.

First Crossing of the Polar Sea

At Chicago our princely journey was over, and as ordinary mortals we stepped on board The Twentieth Century, the most rapid express train in the States. On the 3rd of July at 9 A.M., three hours before the departure of the *Bergensfjord,* we came into New York. Here a splendid reception awaited us, and what in particular moved us deeply here was to see our good friend of Svalbard, Commander Richard Byrd, at the head of the great procession that came with resounding music into the Grand Central Station, and offered us a hearty welcome. It was a glorious close to the splendid triumphal journey through the United States. If we were in doubt as to the feelings of the American people when we reached the west coast, the doubt was amply compensated for by a grand certainty of the whole nation's undivided and warm sympathy and understanding.

It is a pleasure to pass unchecked through the main thoroughfare of a great city, where one otherwise must be content to take his turn like any other mortal and wait until the traffic regulations permit him to cross the street. We drove, at violent speed with a party of police on motor-cycles in front, in the mayoral motor-cars down Fifth Avenue, under the hooting of the sirens. All traffic had to stop, and it was wonderful to see what excellent control the police had over it. On the long way down to the pier of the Norwegian-American Line in Brooklyn, there was not one single sign shown of putting any hindrances in the way of the police. All went with lightning speed. On the company's wharf everything was beautifully decorated and a mass of people had gathered. The Norwegian general-consul, Hans Fay, gave a telling speech and a bower of flowers seemed to surround us. The capital mayoral band had also arrived down here, and the lively American marches sounded through the large building. We were then photographed and filmed, and at last bade farewell. Then came the great moment when one should set foot on Norwegian ground. Some quick steps up the gangway and then one literally fell into the arms of Norway, which at that moment was represented by the *Bergensfjord's* well-known and valued captain, Ole Borneman Bull. He was surrounded by a sea of happy smiling faces, all seeming to shine out a warm welcome. Although all the places had been occupied, the company had sent us a kind invitation and proved better than we can remember on any previous occasion, the truth of the good old saying, "Where there is heart-room, there is house-room."

The homeward voyage with the *Bergensfjord* was one single splendid festivity. All, from the captain to the youngest man, seemed to do their best to spoil us. Thus one day after the other glided by leaving behind a long series of beautiful memories. We had but one regret, and that was that the time went too quickly! On behalf of all of us we thank the Norwegian-American Line for its excellent hospitality and assure them that they have never brought home a flock of more grateful passengers than the crew of the *Norge*.

CHAPTER NINE

Back to Norway

CHAPTER IX

On the 12th of July we came in sight of Norway, two months after our flight over the Pole. We had, whilst still in America, received an invitation from Bergen to be its guests during our stay there. As soon as we had rounded the first little islands we had the feeling of the well-known Bergen hospitality. From every little island and from every house waved the Norwegian flag and everywhere were seen and heard people in festal mood. Cheers rolled like continuous thunder from the drifting fishing-boats to the beflagged town. The weather had appeared doubtful from the morning onwards—indeed, two or three raindrops threatened us even with drizzling weather—but it was only a false alarm. As soon as we came round the last point the sun broke through, and as if by magic there lay one of the most beautiful masterpieces of Norwegian scenery before us, gleaming in all its loveliness. One of our fellow-passengers remarked on the voyage over: "I always have to weep when I come in to Bergen, it is so beautiful." We understood so well this utterance as we stood on the captain's bridge with the old, honored town ahead of us, surrounded

First Crossing of the Polar Sea

by the grand and lofty mountains. Midsummer colors—dark green—had to-day a beautiful woof of red, where the thousand flags were fluttering and flapping in the summer breeze. The Bergenhus fortress gave a salute, the bedecked steamboats hooted and whistled, whilst the boundless mass of people waved up to us. The reception was splendid. The reception committee, headed by the Mayor and the chief magistrate, were the first to bid us welcome. Then came the turn for all the happy "better halves." It is at such a moment that one feels a little out of it, if one does not possess such. But on such a day as this there is not much time for these sentimental reflections. Flowers, cheers, speeches, and the gold chair fill the mind the whole time. After an unforgettable drive through the streets, greeted by the whole population and drowned in a shower of the most exquisite flowers, we were received in a highly ceremonious meeting at the Town Hall and given a welcome. Cameras of all kinds clicked, and the ubiquitous loud speaker gave one the impression of regarding us with extreme compassion: "Poor fellows, what follies will you now commit?" The days in Bergen passed like a delightful dream, and in spite of the want of water, to which they called our attention, we did not for a moment get the opportunity to be thirsty.

What delighted and surprised us still more than the splendid reception was the fine farewell Bergen gave us. A reception is a thing in itself, for then one faces the happy time of music and thoughts of what awaits one brings a smile of joy: "To-night the feast, to-morrow the ball," and so on. It is otherwise with a leave-taking when one is tired and played-out after much festivity. It is rarely that a reception-committee can play their part so well that they are as welcome when they go as when they come. Bergen managed this in a manner we shall never forget. The last glimpse and the last impression that will always endure were of a town and a harbor clad in Norwegian colors.

It was the *Stavangerfjord* that brought us from Bergen to Oslo—once more as the guests of the shipping company. Along the whole coast we noted the same warm-heartedness towards us. Haugesund sent out a large fleet of all kinds of craft with music and cheering; Stavanger, where we stayed two or three hours, invited us to a banquet. The reception and the stay there were in a high degree marked by enthusiastic warmth. The young people of Stavanger had a brilliant idea, having gathered on the quay under banners which in a continuous series represented Amundsen's polar expeditions. First was seen a banner on which the little *Gjöa* was depicted pushing her way through the North-West Passage. On the next was the *Fram* on her way to the South Pole. Then came the *Maud,* broad and solid, on the North-East Passage. On banner number four was seen *N 25* on its flight of a fight with death in 1925, and finally, as a crown to the long labors, the *Norge* in her victorious flight over the North Pole. It was an original, ingenious and beautiful idea of the young folk of Stavanger.

Early next morning we came into Christiansand. It was 5 A.M., so we still lay sleeping when we were suddenly awakened by a well-known and long-missed voice: "Good-day, good-day, and welcome home." And over us, with his brightest smile, stood our friend of the last year's flight, First-Lieutenant Leif Dietrichsen, with a huge bouquet of the finest roses. It was splendid to see him again; we had missed him so often. In the meantime the aeroplanes over the *Stavangerfjord* buzzed a greeting from our War Forces. Masses of boats were out to give us welcome. It really seemed as if we were lazy fellows—but they would forgive us. It is hard work to be a home-coming polar traveler!

The approach to Oslo came in due time under most favorable circumstances in brilliant summer weather. There were flags flying everywhere. At Horten the aviators came out to greet us. They had reason to be proud of the way in which their comrades of the Navy had represented their profession. Farther in came the Military flying men to meet us, and they gave us a very hearty welcome. At 3.30 P.M. the *Stavangerfjord* anchored, and in Mr. Hannibal Fecht's fine motor-cutter we left our popular friend, Captain Irgens, and the many kind passengers. The capital's reception was as unforgettable as it always is, and ended with an audience at the Royal Palace with the King and the Crown Prince. A series of promotions and high decorations were presented to members of the expedition, and the most lasting and best memory was given us: "Our King's satisfaction with our labors."

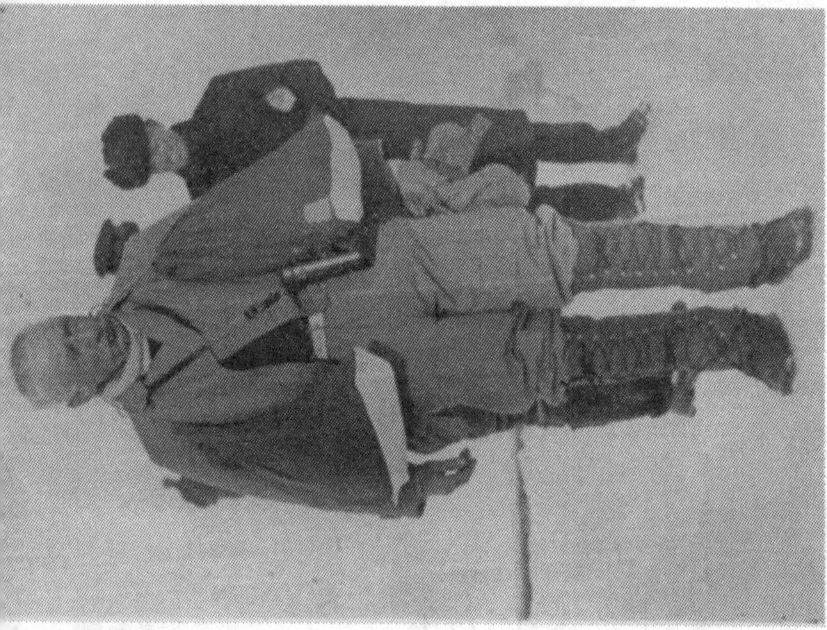

1. SAYING GOOD-BY—A FEW MINUTES BEFORE THE START.

2. OFF FOR ALASKA!

HJ. RIISER-LARSEN

The Navigation Over the Polar Sea

CHAPTER X

THE NAVIGATION OVER THE POLAR SEA

AIR-NAVIGATION

Before I begin to tell of the navigation over the Polar Sea, I will give a short account of the general principles of air navigation and also of the instruments that come into use, so that laymen too may find interest in pursuing the subject.

As in the case of maritime navigation so in air navigation a distinction must be made between terrestrial and astronomical navigation. In the former assistance is found in points on the earth, whilst in the latter the various heavenly bodies are brought into use for the purpose of determining the position. If there is clear weather beneath so that the underlying land—sea or ice—is at all times visible, it is possible, by a careful and incessant calculation of speed and possible drift, to navigate from one point to another without the help of astronomical observations. That is, however, provided that the compasses are quite correct—namely that the exact magnetic variation and deviation are known.

Magnetic variation is the angle between the direction to the geographical pole (the meridian at the place in question) and the needle of the compass. The latter indeed only occasionally points towards the pole mentioned, as the fact is that the *magnetic* pole does not lie at the geographical pole. Many people imagine that this is the case, and have therefore considered our flight to be more hazardous than it really was, as far as navigation was concerned. They have said: "When you reach the North Pole your compass will be useless. How then will you steer forward?" Fortunately it is not so bad as this, and the reason is that the magnetic pole lies on the north coast of Canada and so far away from our route that our compasses would at any time have a strong directional force. There is, however, a peculiarity in magnetic variation that might cause us difficulties in the Polar Sea, where there have not previously been direct magnetic-variations observations taken. The condition is really this: that the compass, apart from a few places, does not point direct to the magnetic pole. It is easy enough to draw up the curves at the places on the earth's surface where one has had occasion to take observations, but up there in the polar basin, we had to sketch in their direction, based exclusively on our judgment. As far as we were concerned there would here come in an uncertainty unless we should get opportunity ourselves to take variation-observations each time, that is, to control the compasses by the position of the sun at the given moment, and, indeed, for that clear weather was required.

The Navigation Over the Polar Sea

I mentioned that it was also an understood thing that we knew the deviation, and I will briefly explain what is meant by this expression.

On board a vessel magnetism will as a rule occur, which exercises its influence upon the compasses so much that they do not show the magnetic north, but are attracted a little away to the one or the other side of this point. This disturbing magnetism may be either permanent magnetism in an object in the vicinity of the compass, or it may be a magnetism that is induced by earth-magnetism in the iron and steel parts of the vessel. It is an easy matter to find the amount of deviation for the various compass-directions, but it is troublesome that this disturbing influence of magnetism varies as one changes the parallel of latitude during the navigating. Thus in Italy, where we corrected the compasses, a fairly small permanent magnet will be of less importance when the horizontal component of the earth's magnetism, that which affects the needle of the compass, is very strong. On high latitudes, where our difficult task lay, this component, however, is naturally very small, which causes a fixed magnet to get a proportionately greater influence. As will appear from what follows we also came to notice this trouble. The same varying influence occurs also with induced magnetism. Consequently in horizontal beams in Italy there will thus be induced a strong magnetism, which will be correspondingly weaker up in the Polar Sea. In the opposite way

the magnetism that is induced in upright constructions by the vertical component of the earth's
magnetism will be weak in Italy and strong in the
Polar Sea.

By calculation of the so-called co-efficients one can
form an idea of how strong influence the various
kinds of magnetism exercise, and take these conditions into consideration, but true enough, not to
a discriminate degree.

The position one thinks one has when navigating
by "clock and compass"—the seaman's popular expression for it—is "dead-reckoning"; the place one
finds by astronomical position-finding is called the
observed position. If one has had another drift,
speed, or course than supposed, one will find this
position by observation, and the one which is correct
does not agree with the position by dead-reckoning.
This difference is called an "error in dead-reckoning." The correcting all the time by drift, speed,
and course is called keeping or maintaining accurate
dead-reckoning. This is much more necessary in the
air than on the sea as the airship, besides moving
forward through the ocean of air, follows the
latter's motion—the wind—in the direction in which
it might blow.

For the purpose of observations of drift there are
to be found a number of instruments which are all
chiefly based on the same principle. We used the
same instrument which we had in the flight in 1925.

namely a Goerz combined drift and speed measure. The instrument is shaped like a telescope and therefore useless in the dark, but is the best I knew for use during the day. During the flight across Europe we used another quite simple instrument at night. Here accuracy in dead-reckoning was not so necessary as with varying intervals we would be able to know points in the country under us.

The Goerz measure was mounted in an opening in the floor of the pilot-gondola and rested here in a bearing on a graduated disc. The method of using it was the following: If the disc is placed on the division O and sight is taken through the glass down to the ground one will see that in the glass there is brought a diametral thread pointing right forward. One then notes that the marked points on the ground one passes directly over follow along the thread. If this be the case one is not exposed to any drifting from the course. That is to say, there is either no wind or a wind direct from ahead or direct from astern. By speed-measurement one will get this point made clear.

If the points mentioned do not follow along the thread, the wind forms an angle with the course and the ship is exposed to drift. Then the glass is turned with or against the hand of the clock, until the objects follow in the direction one proceeds in. The angle between the longitudinal axis of the ship and the direction of the thread, the angle of drift, is then read from the footplate of the instrument. If the angle of drift be small and the wind slight, it is sufficiently correct to steer a corresponding number of degrees up against the wind. If the wind is of any strength and much athwart the course, this procedure is not accurate enough. The direction of the wind in relation to the course will be changed as one luffs to, and as a result of this the angle of drift on the new course will not be the same as before luffing to, and one will not proceed exactly in the direction one supposes.

If we will at once find the right angle we must luff, and at once measure the speed on the old course —that is to say, the speed with which we pass over the ground. This speed is called "maintained speed," in aviation language the expression "ground-speed" is often used. There is a special term for this speed, as it must not be confused with the ship's speed through the air—"air-speed." The air-speed can be read off directly on an instrument which measures the speed of the air-current along the ship, which indeed is the speed of the ship through the air.

With the help of a calculation plate which accompanies the drift-measure, one can then with the angle of drift, ground-speed, and air-speed as basis, at once find the exact angle the course is to be corrected to in order that one can, under the given conditions of weather, proceed in the direction desired.

By calculating it out one gets extra information as to the direction and force of the wind, which is of great interest to the meteorologist.

As the wind usually changes its direction and force with the height above the ground, one must always, if one alters the altitude of the ship, control drift and speed immediately after the alteration. It is also seldom that the wind remains uniform over fairly large areas, even at the same altitude. As one moves with great speed and quickly comes over into new regions, an accurate reckoning on board an airship means, so to speak, an uninterrupted control-measurement of drift and speed.

Drift-measurement over water requires, in general, longer time than over land or ice, as one lacks marked points. If a sea is caused by the wind one will notice that the form of the breakers is lying almost still. Such foam can be used for drift-measurement and, when really large, also for speed-measurement. Over smooth water we used small smoke cartridges fastened to pieces of wood, which we dropped down. At night we could measure by the light from them, and we used them therefore during our passage over the North Sea.

I shall now explain how one measures the ground-speed with the Goerz instrument.

In the lowest part of the instrument, which projects through the bottom of the gondola, a prism is mounted, oscillating round a transverse axis of rotation which, by means of gearing, is connected with a screw with graduations on the top of the instrument. At right-angles on the above-mentioned thread for drift-measuring, there is fastened on the prism a transverse thread. We can therefore see everywhere according to the position of the prism—forward, downward, or astern.

When the speed is to be measured, the instrument is placed on the drift-angle, and the prism is placed on + 45°. When we then look through the glass the sight-line will point 45° across, forward, and downward. At the moment a marked object passes the cross-line, we set a stop-watch going and place the prism back on O, whereby we sight vertically downward. When the object again passes the cross-line we stop the watch. We then have the time the ship takes over a distance corresponding to the ship's altitude above the ground. From a table we then look up the speed. If the ship lies with bow upwards or downwards we must take this angle into consideration. It is not correct to give the steersman orders to keep a horizontal course during the measuring, for then one will, of course, get another speed.

In this measuring there are, however, several sources of making a mistake. Even if the instrument is controlled, and during the measuring we have kept it in the correct position unaffected by the ship's movements, the speed measured will be liable to uncertainty. Thus the steersman will endeavor to keep a steady course both in altitude and sideways during the measuring. Afterwards they will slacken so that the result is that the speed will be less than observed. With such superhumanly long turns at the rudder as our steersman had over the Polar Sea, this difference may reach up to over 5%.

As the measuring, according to the altitude one travels in, takes a certain time—up to a half minute or more—the ship may during this period of time change its altitude. If such change takes place one must use the average altitude in calculating. Besides, it may happen that during the measuring there come squalls, which of course affect the results.

The greatest source of mistake is, however, that the altitude-measure does not show the correct altitude. This measure is an ordinary aneroid barometer, which is placed on O or on the height of the starting-place above sea-level, when the ship, just before the start, is on the ground.

So long as one finds oneself over places with the same barometric pressure as at the starting-place, the altitude-measure shows the correct height. As a rule, however, this pressure will change and thereby one falls into error, which may perhaps be considerable. A change of pressure of 9 mm. will cause an error in altitude of 100 meters, with up to 20% error in the speed measured.

If we find ourselves over regions where meteorological observations are taken that have been transmitted by wireless, we can get our height-measurements corrected. If this be not the case, we must help ourselves in another way.

In measurements of temperature, and the study of meteorological weather-charts which one after another are drawn on board, we can obtain guidance as to what direction the pressure changes to—whether it rises or falls; and also under favorable circumstances a tolerable estimate of the change. Another method of control that can be used during clear weather is to go down at certain intervals to so low an altitude that one can, with some degree of certainty, guess the height. The safest way, of course, is to measure the altitude direct, if this can be done. For use in this respect we took with us an ordinary infantry range-finder with 70 cm. base. A sharp straight line on the ground was required, however, for an accurate measurement. In Italy and during the flight across Europe we had obtained quite good results, for then there were enough "straight lines" to find in railway-lines for instance, footpaths in the streets, and the sides of quays. I had thought that whilst flying over the Polar Sea cracks in the ice might be used, but it proved that the straight-lined cracks with sharp contour appeared so rarely that we had no use for the instrument.

Another method, which may be employed when the sun is high and has such a position that the ship gets a sharp full-length shadow on the ground, is to measure the angle between the bow of the shadow and the stern and also the angle from the vertical to the shadow. The altitude can then be calculated. On account of the low altitude of the sun we could not, however, make use of this method over the Polar Sea. The shadow lay too far away and was not marked enough in its contours.

For the same reason we also could not use the shadow for direct speed-measurement, which otherwise can be done quite simply in the following way: With a stop-watch one measures the time that passes from when the bow of the shadow reaches a marked spot on the ground, and until the after-part of the shadow comes clear of it. During this time the airship has then moved a distance corresponding to its own length.

We still used this method for control of the results we obtained with the Goerz instrument, but it was only a poor control. That the contours are not sharp is the same as saying that the shadow has not its full length. The speed one gets will accordingly be too great. When the speeds obtained by both methods on the whole agreed, we believed the results were correct, and used them for dead-reckoning. Soon, however, we learnt that they were too large: the shadow-method because the contours were not sharp, and the data of the instrument because, amongst other things, the barometric pressure had changed. All observations of latitude were therefore disappointing, as it always proved that we did not stand so far forward, according to the speeds measured, as we should do.

On departure from Italy we had as many as five compasses on board. Three of them were unusable, however, and were discarded one by one. In Pulham we installed on board an English aperiodic compass as a steering-compass. As standard compasses we had, during the polar flight an English aperiodic compass and a German Ludolph compass. We had the same arrangement on N 25 during the expedition in 1925 and our experiences this year coincide with those of last year. It is still impossible for me to say that the one is better than the other. We can, on the other hand, say that the two types complement each other for use there in the north. As a matter of fact, they do not, as a rule, go wrong at the same time. The difference is this, that the aperiodic compass takes a long time to come back to the course if the compass-card has swung out too much on one side, and stops then on the course without the least oscillation, whilst the Ludolph compass comes back rapidly. On the other hand, the latter compass oscillates a long time backwards and forwards on both sides of the course before it comes to rest. Both are equally troublesome when one has little time. The aperiodic compass turned back so slowly that I, in the belief that it had stuck, could have planted my fist on the glass and angrily entreated the compass-card to kindly set itself in motion. Another time I could have clenched my fist at the wildly oscillating Ludolph compass and just as angrily begged it to stop its polkas. In general they behaved well, and should I go the third time I would have the same arrangement. As mentioned above, the two did not indeed have their aberrations at the same time and so we always had one to go by. All airship compasses ought to be provided with jimble suspension with option to lock the rings.

The steering-compass was much interfered with by the fact that the rudder-chain on the side-rudder wheel was extremely magnetic. Even in south latitudes the compass went out 5° when the rudder was turned from the one side to the other. Over the Polar Sea this compass was consequently very uncertain and had, when it was thick weather, to be constantly controlled by the standard compasses, so that the sun-compass could not be used. I thus got a considerable addition to my labors, and I will never go on such a tour again without a rudderchain of non-magnetic material. Once, just after we had passed the ice-pole, we went round in a complete circle, as, being occupied with something else, I had forgotten the compasses.

I now come to the sun-compass, which also was constructed by Goerz. It may be briefly described as a periscope, which is worked by clockwork and which is regulated so that it turns the periscope round at the same time as the sun makes apparently the same movement. If the periscope is directed towards the sun, the reflection of the latter will be cast down on a dull glass-plate, on which there is a wire cross marked. When the compass is adjusted for the course required, the steersman's duty is always to keep the reflected image in its place. This task is not difficult. It is thus much easier to steer by the sun-compass than by a magnetic one. Adjustment must be made for the sun's declination at the time concerned, just as one must correct for change of latitude, as the axis of the periscope must always be parallel with the axis of the earth. If such an adjustment or correction be not taken, one will not get the sun's image to follow the horizontal thread of the wire cross already mentioned. The image will move parallel to this either over or under, and at a distance from it corresponding to the error in the adjustment. The instrument is so sensitive that it can also be used for determining the latitude, when the declination and the longitude are known.

On the outer side of the gondola, opposite the side-rudder steersman, there was placed an outrigger for fixing up the sun-compass. In order that this might have free play as the sun was on one side or the other, there was an outrigger on the port-side and one on the starboard-side. It was the

1. THE "NORGE" OFF ON HER LONG JOURNEY.

2. LOOKING DOWN ON KING'S BAY (600 MILES FROM THE NORTH POLE).

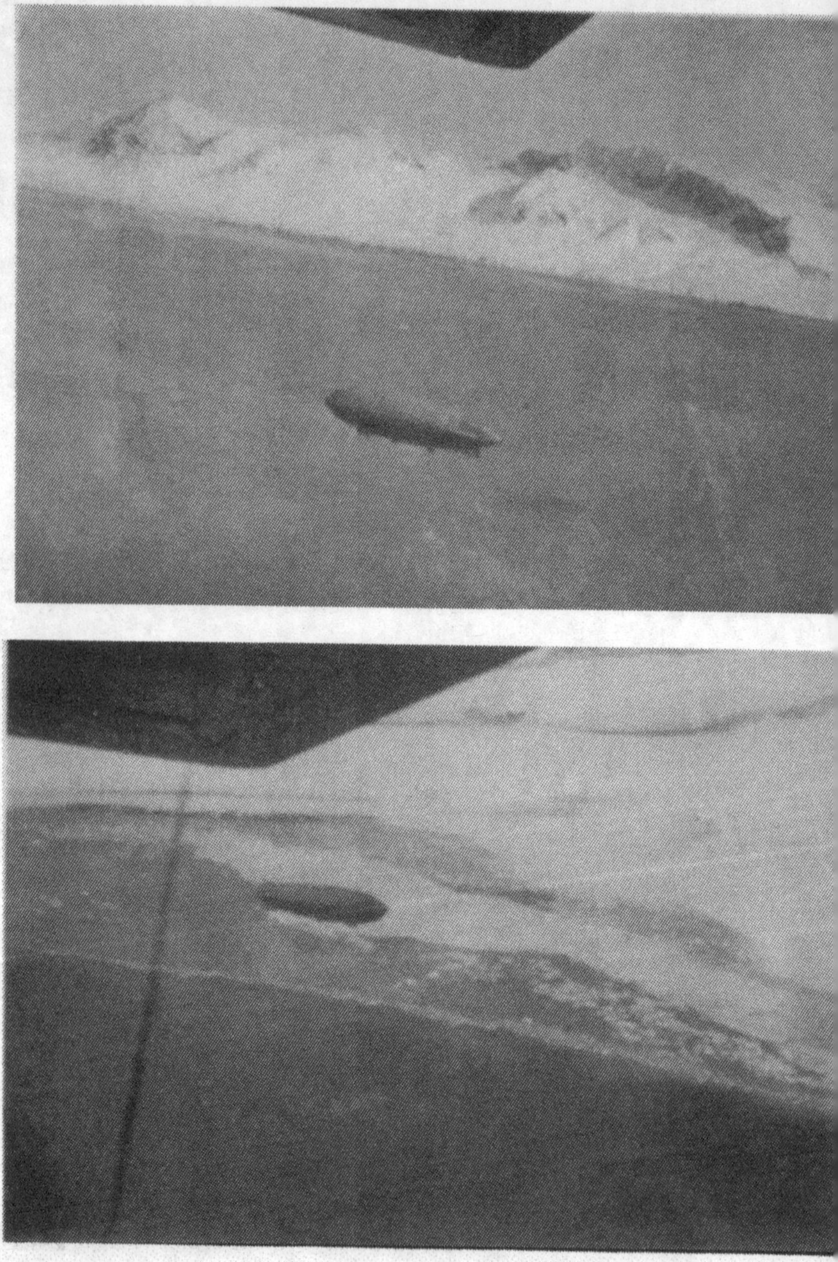

"NORGE" ON HER WAY—TAKEN FROM COMMANDER BYRD'S PLANE.

navigator's most unpleasant job to shift the compass from one side to the other, as this must be done with half his body outside the gondola in an 80-kilometer wind. Another time I shall know how to arrange the shifting in a far more practical way. To manipulate small screws in such a wind and at such a temperature is no agreeable task.

For the calculation of the sun's altitude we had a sextant of German make with artificial horizon on it. It was one of the best sextants I have ever used. It was easy to manipulate and gave surprisingly accurate results.

As to the chronometers, Amundsen and Ellsworth had made careful comparisons between them for a fairly long period. They were kept during the flight preserved at the same temperature as on land. As appears from Amundsen's account, they were also controlled during the flight by time-signals through the radio-station.

We used charts on Mercator's projection right up to 80° north on the Spitsbergen side, and to 75° north on the Alaska side of the North Pole. North of these parallels we had charts on the gnomonic projection. In addition, we had a set of special charts for coast-regions around the whole polar basin in case we should be obliged to seek the nearest land. For this purpose Amundsen had also procured a list of all depots to be found there, so that we could select the most favorable way of escape, if conditions should make it impossible for us to reach the north coast of Alaska. Amundsen had determined, in such a case, to make for Patrick Island. Strong north-easterly winds might, however, also have forced us over to the Siberian coast. As Wisting had just come from these regions he was fully cognizant of what there was to fall upon there.

Of almanacs we used the Nautical Almanac and the Norwegian Fishery Almanac. The latter is the only almanac which gives azimuths to 90° north latitude. With the possibility of wintering there before us, we had also almanacs for 1927!

In order that one can more easily understand what follows, I will endeavor to briefly explain astronomic navigation. A single calculation of the altitude of a heavenly body does not give immediate information as to what point on the globe one is placed. Unfortunately it is not so simple as that. One gets to know merely that one is on some spot on a small circle, whose center is that point which at the moment has the heavenly body in question in zenith and whose radius is equal to 90°, minus the calculated altitude of the heavenly body. This circle is called the position-circle. To construct this position-circle would be troublesome, but it is fortunately not necessary. In ordinary navigation the error in reckoning will not be greater than that it is accurate enough to calculate a tangent to the circle named. Thus one gets by a single observation information that one is at one place or another on a line called the position-line. If one wishes to know at once exactly where one is, one must, if conditions permit, immediately after the first observation, calculate also the altitude of another heavenly body which is found well out to the side of the first. Where the two position-lines intersect is the point where one is.

In the daytime, one as a rule refers to the sun alone and has then nothing to do but wait a certain time until the sun has changed its position so far that one can by an observation, No. 2, get a position-line which gives good intersection with the one from which the first observation was obtained.

If during this time of waiting one is in the same place the case is simple, but is a little complicated if one has moved. If one has been able, during the time of waiting (which should be about three hours), to keep quite accurate dead-reckoning, there is no inexactitude. Then one has to move the first position-line parallel to itself in the direction of the course with a distance corresponding to the distance sailed in the intervening time. The point of inter-section of the position-lines is then the observed point by the last observation. When the speed is comparatively small as in sea navigation the error can never be great. In air navigation, where the speed is great and difficult to calculate, just under those very conditions where one desires exactitude, one has little satisfaction in coupling two observations with so long an interval. I refer here to navigation over clouds and fog when one cannot take calculations of ground-speed and drift. Over Alaska we found ourselves unable to take observations in a wind of about 80 kilometers per hour. If we had moved such a position-line we should, after the required time-interval, have placed this line more than 200 kilometers outside its correct position. In that case the method was therefore quite impracticable.

As it was quite impossible to keep the exact reckoning, we never coupled the position-lines together. We calculated when the sun would be in meridian on that place we were, and at that moment took an observation, whether at noon or at midnight. It gave us a position-line going east-west, and consequently the latitude. In the same way we calculated the moment the sun was due east or west and got a position-line in north-south direction, which gave us the longitude. We also took observations outside these times but used them only as guidance.

I will also briefly mention the calculation of an observation. In the vicinity of the Pole, that is, north of 85° north latitude, there is so slight a difference in the hour-angle (direction to the sun from the polar point) and azimuth (direction to the sun from the place occupied) that one can reduce the whole calculation to a simple and rapid operation. One notes the time and finds what meridian the sun was on at the moment; the declination is drawn from the altitude measured. The difference is set out from the Pole towards the sun if the difference is positive, from the sun if it be negative. At this distance from the Pole, one draws a line perpendicular to the meridian and thereby one has the position-line.

South of 85° this method becomes inexact and therefore we have used St. Hilaire's method (altitude method). By this one calculates the position and then calculates what altitude the sun should have had over the horizon if one had found oneself to be on this spot. The difference between this and the actual measured altitude is called the altitude-error. One then reckons out the true direction to the sun from the position, puts this in on the chart, and constructs the position-line perpendicular to the same at a distance from the place occupied corresponding to the difference in altitude. This will then be the position-line where one must have been placed according to the measured altitude.

I mentioned above that by day "as a rule" one has the sun only for use for astronomical calculations of position. The exception is the periods when the moon is up at the same time as the sun. The moon is, however, a very uncertain friend, who only plays a visitor's part. When she is north she has much too great speed work to come south again. Still no such visitor-rôle took place at the time of our flight. We had therefore only the sun, and it may be unnecessary to relate that the reason is that in polar regions in summer the day is both night and day. At the Pole the year has only one day and night so far as light and darkness are concerned. The day lasts exactly six months; the other six are night. If one be entirely theoretic, then ever since the earth existed it has always been noon at the polar point itself, because the sun has always stood due south. Naturally all directions lead south. When I say that it is necessary to call attention to this condition, my reason is that, shortly before departure from Spitsbergen, we received a telegram from one who should, to judge from his position, know better—I will not mention his name—who wished us a prosperous voyage in "the everlasting night." And Amundsen has had much amusement from a complimentary poem that begins: "From North Pole's cold to South Pole's warmth."

It was as to how we navigated across the Polar Sea that I should particularly write of, and I admit at once that this is a rather long introduction. Many who read it will say: "How he has drawn it out." But it is not for these readers I have written. Most of those who read this book are not expert in navigation and would have found little or no pleasure in reading about the navigation itself had

The Navigation Over the Polar Sea

I gone direct to it without these explanations. If they have aroused interest in those who know nothing of navigation then my purpose is fulfilled.

THE VOYAGE [1]

It was 8.55 A.M. on the 11th of May when the *Norge* slowly rose into the brilliantly clear air. The whole of the wonderfully beautiful snow-clad land lay bathed in sunshine beneath us. Below stood all our friends, waving to us as long as we could see them. Their firm grips of the hand at starting had betrayed a certain anxiety, and now they stood with minds full of an ardent hope that all might go well with us. In our own thoughts there was no room for any anxiety. We were entirely filled with a feeling of relief—an extraordinary joy that at last we were off. Thoughts went back to days, one year previously, when we waited for good weather in order to go northward with flying-machines. At that time it was only to the region towards the North Pole that we should explore. Our resources had not allowed us to equip an expedition for solving the original problem, Amundsen's great aim for many years—the exploration of the Polar Sea right over to Alaska. Therefore Amundsen called last year's expedition a reconnoitering expedition.

At that time everything was ready for starting;

---

[1] All hours referred to are Greenwich Mean Time.

we had nothing to do but wait; but this is characteristic of how full of his problem Amundsen was, that, just before the venture, of which no one could say what the result would be, he set about making plans for this expedition which we now set out on. Year after year he had labored towards this goal, had suffered disappointments and privations—but, no, I cannot bear to stir up again the troubles he had to endure. But now he stood there free and happy, and looked northward whilst the west coast of Svalbard glided past us. I too was glad that I had got my mite to offer. In 1921 I had been trained as airship-pilot in England, the reason alone being that I might with so much greater authority be able to work at home for an airship-route: London—Oslo—Stockholm—Leningrad. After I had been thrown out of a number of financiers' offices with my plans, I had come exactly as far as when I first began with the route, and the money I had used on it was thrown away. Still, this affair was in no little degree the cause of our now finding ourselves here. How little one suspects!

But now we were steering northwards, and nothing could stop us. The voyage from Rome to Svalbard had been quite exciting—and just for this reason, that a possible disaster would have stopped the expedition. I will in this connection avail myself of the opportunity of correcting a misunderstanding that I have since become aware of. It has been said that the most risky part of the expedition was the flight to Svalbard. When that had been accomplished the rest of the expedition would also succeed. It has been explained in this way that the flight from Rome to Svalbard was more dangerous than the flight from Svalbard to Alaska. It is, of course, an incorrect interpretation. By this statement was only meant that the long flight to Svalbard held a great risk to the expedition. Should anything go wrong with the ship, the whole expedition, indeed, would be upset. Therefore our first plans were to equip a mother-vessel for the airship, by which the latter could be freighted to Svalbard. When we were once there, nothing could stop us. For the crew there was only inconsiderable risk in that flight, whilst it cannot, of course, be denied that there was great risk connected with the second flight, the real expedition.

At 10 o'clock we were across Magdalene Bay, and steered in to an overland mark in order to control the deviation of the compasses. Twenty-seven minutes later we had the north point of Amsterdam Island abeam, and we drew a little eastward so as to come into the meridian of King's Bay radio-station, as we should then take radio-bearings right astern of this station. Immediately afterwards the ice-edge was passed. Before us lay all the snow-decked ice-field of the Polar Sea, glittering in the sunshine. It was exactly ten days short of one year since the last time we steered northward.

At the beginning we went at only 200 meters altitude, and had the stern and port motors each going at 1,200 revolutions. This would give an air-speed of 80 kilometers. Drift-measurements were steadily taken as the north-easterly wind increased by degrees. As the speed over the ground had come down to 72 kilometers, with up to 30° drift to the port side, we agreed, after a conference with Malmgren, to rise to a higher altitude. With constant calculations of speed, the height was then increased to 530 meters, where, with 14° drift to the same side, we got a ground-speed of 86 kilometers: at that height the wind was abaft the beam, and thus helped us forward. As the drift varied, the course was changed. If it were only a few degrees change to be made, the steersman received orders to keep the image of the sun in the sun-compass a corresponding number of degrees to the side of the center of the cross-thread. If there were greater variations, the adjustment of the compass was amended.

As often as there was an opportunity, Gottwaldt took radio-bearings of King's Bay. At 14 o'clock we got a bearing which showed that we were a little east of dead-reckoning. As will be seen from the chart, a new course was set. The routine which was followed was this: The navigator gave his orders direct to the side-helmsman. If he found that the speed, on account of contrary wind, decreased too much, he conferred with the meteorologist and the pilot on duty, and also with the leaders. If the pilot in question then found that there was nothing in the way, from a gas-technique point of view, to prevent attempting a great altitude, and the leaders (from the point of view of observation) had no objection, the pilot gave his orders to the main steersman. They then tried, as mentioned above, to reach an altitude in which they got the best speed.

The result of the various measurings and calculations of position were announced in turn to the leaders and to the pilot of the ship. It simplified the matter that the second-in-command of the expedition and the navigator were one and the same person, and it was still more simple when he was also the pilot on duty. The fact that the crew was so small brought, however, increased work on Nobile, as I could not, according to the original plan, undertake the fourth task of also being the second-in-command of the ship and attending to the duties connected with that position. Nobile had, therefore, to undertake the various rounds of inspection in order to see that everything was in order, and that there were no errors cropping up. The intention had also been that Nobile and I should go on watch turn and turn about. As the crew was now, I should, however, get all the navigation without an opportunity of sleep, and should, as a result of the burden of work, be also unable to undertake the regular watch as pilot. This also affected Nobile's chances of getting the necessary sleep, which was reduced considerably.

If the weather conditions would be such that the risk might arise of not being able to reach Alaska, so that there might be a question of returning or of making towards Canada or Siberia, the decision on this point would be left to the two leaders of the expedition, the second-in-command, and the ship's pilot in common. Fortunately no such situation arose.

From 16 o'clock onwards no drift was measured, so that we could point to the bow just as to the Pole. An observation of the sun at 17 o'clock showed that we were back on King's Bay meridian.

At 18:30 o'clock we came into wind which caused us a little drifting to starboard, but it was fortunately astern and slightly increased our speed.

At 18.40 the port-side motor was stopped, as it had lately gone unevenly on account of defective petrol-supply. We continued with the stern motor alone, with about 55 kilometers speed, until we had got the starboard motor going. During the warming up of this we kept it going with only 1,000 revolutions, and therefore had for a time only 70 kilometers speed. But what a wonderful sense of safety we had in being on board an airship and not in a flying-machine. If the motors stopped we did not, indeed, require to land. The fault in the supply of petrol to the port-side motor was remedied. Some water had come into one of the pipes and had frozen. At 19:55 this was going again and the starboard motor was stopped.

Whilst the stern motor was going on the whole flight, one of the side-motors was stopped as reserve. The most economic speed—that is to say, the speed with which we could sail farthest with our supply of petrol—was, as a matter of fact 80 kilometers, which could be attained with two motors at 1,200 revolutions. The maximum number of revolutions for the motors was 1,400, and therefore 1,200 was not any particularly great strain.

At 19:30 it clouded over. Until then we had had brilliant sunshine from a cloudless sky, and had the whole time been able to steer by the sun-compass. The drift to starboard increased to 12°, and the speed was occasionally down to 60 kilometers.

At 22:25 the fog was as thick as a wall right ahead. We rose to an altitude of 1,000 meters, and proceeded in over the sea of fog, steering by the solar-compass. The last calculation before the ice disappeared from under us gave no drift and a speed of 67 kilometers.

At midnight by King's Bay meridian we took a midnight observation, which gave us a latitude of

88° 30′. This observation was very convenient, as it gave us opportunity of verifying our speed. As the ice lay concealed, we could not indeed take direct speed calculations. It was clear that we had calculated too great a speed previously, and the reason probably was that the altitude-measurer showed an error. According to the radio-bearings, we found ourselves now to be steadily on the right meridian. This was supported by the fact that we had the sun right ahead exactly at midnight. There was still some trouble with the port motor a few times, and therefore we had the starboard motor going for a while.

There was, now and then, opportunity to measure drift and speed, through openings in the coverings of cloud. There was a light head-wind right against the prow. It was fortunate that it came straight against the prow, as there was then no difficulty in keeping on the meridian with course due north, so long as we could use the solar-compass. During the whole voyage the solar-compasses had acted well. There is really on that course little magnetic variation, but now we began to come in over regions where it quickly changed its value.

At 1 o'clock of the night before the 12th it speedily cleared up below us. Needless to say, we were all glad of this. It would have been a disappointment not to see the "top of the world." After having carefully verified the speed-measurements,

we ought to find ourselves over the polar point at
1:30. At 1 o'clock therefore I calculated the altitude the sun would have on the sextant at the
point of time when we were at the Pole. The sextant was adjusted, and I began to take the altitude
of the sun, which steadily came nearer, its image
on the sextant.

At 1:15 I went down on my knees and measured
steadily out through one of the portholes whose
coverings had been removed. When the reflection
of the sun and the bubble for the artificial horizon
lay side by side, sharply touched by the marking-
threads, I announced: "Now we are there." The
time was 1:25. Under us lay the polar basin,
bathed in sunshine. We slackened speed, and went
down to 200 meters altitude. One by one the flags
were dropped down, whilst we stood with uncovered
heads. Thanks to the special way in which the flags
had been fastened to the poles, they went beautifully
down, and with good enough speed for the steel
points to penetrate the snow and ice. The colors
streamed out nicely as the flags flew down. When
the ceremony was over all our hands sought Amundsen's, and then, naturally enough, Wisting's. There
stood the only two men who had planted their
country's flag at both Poles. And they were Norwegians.

We made a short circle round the polar area. The
course was set so much to the left as is the difference

between the meridian of King's Bay and that of Point Barrow, and speed was put on the motors again.

In addition to keeping the calculation of time according to Greenwich, we had also, with regard to observations, to make a calculation of the time by the meridian concerned on which we were.

As previously stated, we could then take observations when the sun was in a position favorable for determining the latitude and longitude.

But at Point Barrow the time is about ten and a half hours after the time at Greenwich, and about eleven hours after King's Bay time. The moment we had crossed the Pole it was not the 12th of May any longer, but the afternoon of the 11th of May. We experienced two evenings consecutively without the intervening time. Ellsworth's birthday was thus not very long, but he consoled himself with the fact that he could begin it again in a few hours.

Now we began our special task, the exploration of the endless stretch from the Pole to Alaska. It is not indeed endless, but I remember that I thought it was a very long distance when I looked at the chart.

And how would it go with sleepiness? It was a pity we had not had our fill of sleep when we started from Svalbard. The mechanics had had hard work getting the motors ready. On the flight to the north the port-side motor had been damaged over Kirkeness, and a new one had been put in at Spitsbergen. There had, of course, been a whole lot of other preparations. For my own part, I had slept three hours on the night before the start.

It was also tiring for us that the accommodation on board was so poor. The place was so small that we could not take a full step to any side. As navigator I had constantly to move about between the steering-compass and the solar-compass forward and the drift-measure astern. It was an unceasing twist backwards and forwards. Fortunately the temperature was not lower than 13° centigrade below zero. Had I had to have my flying-dress on, it would undoubtedly have been beyond a joke. If I in my haste pressed a little too hard on any one who was planted too firmly, then I hereby beg his pardon for it.

That bunks had not been fixed up on board was not so great a point, as we, on account of want of relief from duties, became so tired at the end that we could stand upright and sleep.

The meals were not very happy moments, either. An exhaust-cooker that had been lent to us in England, and which had been used with great success on R 34's fine flight to and from America, was unfortunately not mounted. We had therefore to resort to coffee and tea from thermos-flasks, which were already rather cold. The sandwiches were ice-cold and like bits of wood to bite. The meat-cakes consisted entirely of ice-crystals. As far as I was concerned, I thawed them in my trouser-pockets.

From 2.15 on the 12th it was slightly clouded occasionally, and at such periods we steered by the magnetic compass. At 4 o'clock I again noted sunshine. The course corresponded with the solar-compass.

At 4.20 we took an observation that showed we steered a little west of dead-reckoning. From that time onwards there was a slight drift to port, without, however, any decrease of speed. The altitude varied between 600 and 700 meters.

The magnetic variation now shifted steadily away from its value, and therefore the course had to be constantly changed so that we could keep on our meridian.

This was very troublesome, as I did not feel quite safe in relying on the chart. At 6 o'clock, when we could compare with the solar-compass, I entered in the log: "The magnetic variation appears to be 10° less than the chart gives."

At 7 o'clock I took the last drift-observation for a spell. We then ran into a fog a little while later. If I am to be perfectly honest, I really had no objection to this, for it gave me, as a matter of fact, an opportunity to sit down for the first time since leaving King's Bay.

I got a nap of half an hour, which refreshed me. I awoke on hearing that the ice could be seen and so

I could continue my measurings. It was indeed only in glimpses we saw it then.

At 10.45 the port motor had to be stopped on account of a broken valve-spring. The starboard motor was set going whilst a new spring was put in.

We constantly found ourselves over fog. The old theory that in the Polar Sea early in the summer the fog would never extend over great areas received a "shot between wind and water." Fortunately there were openings in the fog covering at short intervals, both under and out to the side of us, and this made it possible to verify that there was only sea.

At 17.19 we had a little sensation. Westward there sprang up something out of the fog that looked like a mountain-ridge. We had often seen a "Cape Fly-away" without being fooled by it, for as a rule the contours will change a little whilst one is looking. Both Amundsen and I stood for a time and regarded this land. As there was no variation whatever the helm was put up, and in great suspense we steered towards it. It was not, however, long before we were aware that this too was a "Cape Fly-away," for in the log I have under the time of 17.30 noted: "Back on course."

Some time later it clouded over, and we could only steer by the magnetic compasses. Fortunately for me, we were then outside the region where the magnetic variation so constantly changed. We could now keep the same course for a fairly long time at a stretch. But ahead of us it darkened little by little. The fog under us grew higher, and it was necessary for us to steadily rise in order to keep above it; whilst the roof of clouds above us came steadily lower and lower. I was at this time also on watch as pilot, and I endeavored to come up over the layer of cloud, as I discovered that not far ahead it joined with the fog below. As we were up at 1,100 meters altitude, and still had far to go, I had to give it up. We could not, indeed, proceed higher without letting out gas. As is known, this expands as the air-pressure decreases with the higher altitude. We would not necessarily let out any gas before it was absolutely needful. If we got formation of ice on the ship we would be glad of every single cubic meter.

We then made downwards again through clearings in the fog; there were constantly openings through which we could see the ice. Nobile now came on watch, and we both agreed to go down to quite a low altitude, as it might happen that the fog did not lie right down to the ice. The going down proceeded quite slowly, so that the balloonettes could be filled by degrees.

Under the gas-bags there are, as a matter of fact, some air-bags (balloonettes), which are filled with air from an opening in the bow. As the gas is contracted under the increasing air-pressure whilst descending, its diminution must be replaced in volume by an increasing air-volume in the balloonettes. In this way the ship is always kept full under a pressure a little higher than the external air-pressure. Thus do non-rigid and semi-rigid airships keep their shape.

We at once discovered that during this time ice had begun to form on the projecting metal sections, the rope-work, and the sides of the gondolas. This was what we had feared, and it made us determined to look for clear weather below, if lower down conditions should be such. For a moment it looked promising, until we found, farther on, that the clouds, true enough, did not come right down to the ice, but that, instead, it was snowing quite hard. The formation of ice on the ship increased. After a conference with Malmgren we agreed to go up again. Malmgren opened one of the port-holes and took temperature and vapor measurements incessantly. And so by degrees we endeavored to increase our altitude.

I cannot deny that we thought the situation rather serious. Still, it might have been worse. The formation of ice decreased a little, but not entirely. We therefore made a new attempt to come over the layer of cloud, but it lay too high up, and we sought therefore to come down to the altitude where the formation of ice was least.

The solar-compass froze to a solid block of ice of fantastic shape, and of course stopped working.

The other metal sections fitted outboard on the motor-gondolas got a layer of ice. The guys that were hanging down along the sides and were of wire became bars of ice an inch thick, and the rope guys got a coating of coarse rime-crystals. The canvas on the pilot-gondola and the canvas over the whole bow-construction of the ship got a coating of fine rime, whilst the canvas on the balloon-covering itself, which was encased with rubber (rubbered) was unaffected. From this it seems that ice is directly proportional to the heat-conducting capacity of the object in question. Pure ice settled on metal-work, white frost on rope-work and ordinary canvas, whilst the rubberized canvas was unaffected.

On future flights to this region all external canvas ought therefore to be rubberized. All projecting metal-sections ought to be covered with such canvas, and all guys should be able to be hauled in on board. Moreover, the gas-valves and balloonette filling-valves for ships of this type ought to be of such dimensions that the ship can quickly be taken up to a very high altitude in order to get into clear weather. I am aware that to use rubberized canvas as covering for the cases will involve a very great difference in weight for rigid airships. The gas is in these in special gas-bags, whilst the case is the only covering outside the rigid construction, going over and round the whole ship. This case need not be gas-tight, and is therefore made of an ordinary light canvas. As far as these ships are concerned one ought to find, by means of careful tests, a canvas and a glazing that will not be liable to the formation of rime.

Calamities now seriously commenced. As the guys slung backwards and forwards under the motions of the ship, pieces of ice broke off and fell down. The pieces of ice from the guys which were near the front of the propellers on the side-gondolas, together with pieces of ice from the gondolas themselves, sometimes got into the propeller, and became like small projectiles from a machine-gun slung out to the side with violent force. Some of them were slung through the canvas into the keelson, and several of these made holes in the bottom of the balloonettes. Our splendid mechanics were, therefore, under the prominent leadership of Cecioni, constantly occupied in putting patches on the holes. It sounded like the sharp crack of a gun when these projectiles went through. It was extremely disconcerting. For a long time we went at slow speed so that the velocity of the "projectiles" should not be so great. It was a good thing that the envelope of the gas-bags themselves had been strengthened in the vicinity of the propellers. No projectiles penetrated there, but we really could not know how long that would be so.

We endeavored to hold our course as well as possible, so as to keep on the meridian of Point Barrow.

As will appear from Malmgren's account, the reception of meteorological reports ceased, and Gottwaldt will explain the reason for this. The speed was extremely irregular; there was no opportunity for speed- and drift-measurements. The openings we saw under us were so small that we passed too rapidly over them. We saw nothing of the sun, therefore the whole of the reckoning had to be based exclusively on one's own judgment. Fortunately Malmgren could, on the basis of the old reports and of his own observations, draw up a kind of chart, which showed that we should probably get a steadily increasing east wind that would turn northwards little by little as we approached Point Barrow. That chart became of invaluable use to me. We therefore turned the course by degrees a little eastward, so as to keep up against the increasing wind, and so hope for a glimpse of the sun when we got it in a favorable position for a determination of longitude. In the case of latitude it was indeed not so dangerous, owing to the north coast of Alaska being very low.

Once we had such a large rent in the canvas that we had to slow down, whilst it was repaired, to the least possible speed compatible with steering. We then chanced to come out over the ice at quite a low altitude, and found that the clouds farther in front were not lying very low. Whilst the repairs were proceeding we regarded the ice under us, but no longer with purely platonic glances. We now discussed what the ice would be like to walk on, should the ship, through excessive weight caused by ice, be forced to land, and we be compelled to continue our journey on foot. It would be a long distance to go, and the ice was treacherous.

Some time later we glided forwards again, and found to our great joy that, by keeping 100 or 150 meters altitude, we were clear of the curtain of clouds. Gradually it became lighter in front, and our spirits rose. Now and then the sun shone through and gave me—immediately after 3.20 on the 13th of May (at which time dead-reckoning position observed is entered on the chart)—an observation which showed that we had not really steered up so much eastward as supposed. With the port motor going and the starboard one stopped, the ship had a tendency to draw to the starboard and westward. We got a position-line very nearly parallel with our course which cut the coast a little west of Point Barrow. We were placed somewhere at a point on this line, but how far from the coast?

The speed we had not really been able to keep control of. I had to take it on my own judgment, and estimated it a little substantially for the purpose of beginning to navigate with care in good time, in case the fog should draw down to the ice again. The position that is marked on the new line at 4 o'clock is therefore the nearest we could be to land.

I could, almost with certainty, therefore, say that we were not so near, but could not say how far away we were. To set out the new course for Point Barrow would accordingly be absolute guesswork. It was not of interest, either, as, with our large stock of petrol remaining, we should of course continue southward, so as, if possible, to reach the region so near Nome that we could get the first boat south that goes from there in June. We had thus nothing to do with Point Barrow, and the only logical thing was to set a course along the position-line so that we could make land there where it cuts the coast.

This we did, but it was some time before there was anything to see. It was clear we had stood farther from land at 4 o'clock than was entered on the chart. So as not to arouse nervousness I calculated when we would sight land according to the greatest and lowest speed calculated by the time from the last observation on latitude on 76° 46'. It would be at the earliest 6 o'clock, and at the latest 8 o'clock. The time was a little over 6.30 when there began to take shape some dark points on the port bow and right ahead. I dared not for the time being say anything, so as not to disappoint any one, for "Land ahead" meant everything to us.

The points widened by degrees to narrow strips with white incisions in them. At 6.45 I was certain of my point, and announced: "Land ahead and on the port bow." The announcement ran like wildfire from gondola to gondola. There were smiles on every face and an eager stare towards the black thing ahead that grew larger. Nobile pulled out his egg-brandy, and gave me a tot which I can still taste. The course was laid more eastward so as to come nearer land, but it took time, as the wind was easterly and rather fresh.

At 7.25, forty-six hours and twenty minutes after we left the ground at King's Bay, we came in over the land—and the Polar Sea had been crossed for the first time.

But where were we? Special charts were already produced, but it was impossible to pick out the run of the coastline. There were indeed such extremely weak contours on the shore and shallow so far, that it was quite impossible to decide on the snow-covered ice where the coastline went. The black things we saw were some gravel-heaps in on the land, and behind these lay the snow-covered land—flat as far as we could see in the misty air.

There was nothing else to do but follow the coast until we came to a fairly large place of habitation where we could get assistance. Amundsen followed the coast with rapt attention until we came to Wainwright, which he at once recognized. By making up the dead-reckoning back again we were able to ascertain that we really had cut the coast as we had previously conjectured—namely just west of Point

Barrow. We later got confirmation of this, as we had been observed from there.

How we now longed for meteorological reports! Along the coast the weather did not look promising, and it might happen that it would be better in the direction of Fairbanks, from whence we could obtain connection southward. Now we knew nothing, and, with such visibility, there could be no thought of trying to go forward over the mountains in that direction. It would be better to follow the coast as well as we could.

I had looked forward to a little rest now that we had come to the coast and had decided where we were. In clear weather the further part of the task would have been simple, but unfortunately it steadily thickened, and it proved that the remaining part of the navigation would be a more difficult problem than the navigation over the Polar Sea.

If only we had had more coffee! The last cold drop had been drunk long ago. There was no more to brace oneself up with. The only thing that kept me up to the mark was the difficulty of finding the way forward.

As we approached Cape Lisburne the fog lay so low that the flight began to become rather sinister. We went quite low—so low that Wisting at the main-rudder had to show the greatest resource to keep the ski clear of the ice under us. Horgen stood by the side-rudder equally watchful, so as not to come too near the ridge of land or too far from it so that we should lose it from sight. A gale blew behind us, so that we made great speed, which, of course, increased the risk. As pilot in charge I dared not, at last, continue longer at this low altitude. Against my will, however, it was necessary to enter the fog, and so lose the lay of the land— still, there was no other way of escape. We went up, and came on over the layer of clouds into brilliant sunshine. But on all sides there was an endless curtain of cloud. We were now in the vicinity of the mountainous region, but not a mountain-top reached above the clouds. Through a rift in the clouds we some time later saw that we were over land. Nobile had again taken over the watch, and I concentrated on the navigation. It was impossible to recognize any of the broken mountainsides over which we passed. But this much we learnt from them: that there was a very fresh north-west wind blowing. We therefore set a westerly course, so to come out over Bering Strait again. Then it opened under us, and we went down through such an opening to try to make progress under the covering of clouds. It went well for a time. We followed a mountain-ravine southward, with the mountains on both sides reaching up to the clouds. The direction of the wind was partly across the ravine, and therefore we had a good deal of rolling.

There we saw a little of a river, which we by mistake supposed to be one which lay considerably farther south. Immediately after, the way was barred by heavy black clouds, and we again steered aloft and came into sunshine, but with the whole land shut out beneath us. Now there was nothing to do but keep a course so westerly that we were sure to come out over Bering Strait. It would take time, and gave me the opportunity for a very necessary half-hour's sleep. And so on again once more.

Towards 16 o'clock we now agreed that we could continue no farther, for there was no end to the covering of clouds. But to be resigned to going down through the fog, without further consideration and quite ignorant of where we were, was the act of a madman. We might just as well find ourselves over the sea, and so would not risk anything by going carefully down, as we indeed might find that we were over land, which in this locality had mountains more than a thousand meters high, with clouds lying like thick wool right into the mountain-wall. This we had indeed observed before we rose over the clouds the last time. The result of a collision with a mountain-wall under these conditions of weather would be apparent.

We therefore proceeded with observation of the sun, and at 16 o'clock got a position-line, which from the chart can be seen to cut over Seward Peninsula. The lines of the course on the chart were drawn up in such a way that afterwards we could see that they must have been accurate. At that time we did not know where on the line we were; we could, as mentioned before, have well been over land. At 17.45 we got a position-line which went due north and south through Bering Strait and clear of land. The danger was thereby over.

We then set a course northward, so that by going against the wind we might get up a little speed. The bow was pointed downward; the bow-valve was opened fully to let air into the balloonettes, and we sank slowly and carefully down through the fog. On all sides everything looked like white wool. It was some time before we could go carefully forward. Then at last it was a little brighter beneath us, and soon after we proceeded over the ice. To our great delight we found that the fog did not lie quite down to the ice. By flying cautiously we should be able to see a little when we kept quite low. A rather fresh breeze, however, was blowing.

During the extremely long time we had been in the fog since we first entered it in the polar ice I, of course, had missed Gottwaldt's excellent radio-bearings. Gottwaldt has explained how the wireless came to be silenced.

But we had not yet come down to the ice, and were just beginning to calculate how far south or north we now were when Gottwaldt came running to say he heard a station and had got its bearings. It corresponded with another station without his having been able to get the opportunity of hearing its name. Gottwaldt thought that it was possibly Nome, but it might easily have been some other station. I, at any rate, made out this bearing for Nome, and could now set a course south-east to Cape Prince of Wales.

During the flight down through the fog the ice had begun to form, and continued to do so; projectiles again flew into the ship. Nobile then came with the alarming announcement that all material for patching up the holes had been used up, and that the ship was in such condition that we must do our best to make the nearest land, wherever it might be, and as soon as possible.

However, little by little as we got away from the ice-rim, the ice came to an end, and we found ourselves over the open sea, with the waves increasing in the stiff gale. Then the question arose as to whether the radio-station was really Nome or one farther south. It was possible that there was no more ice southward. If we should find ourselves south of Diomede Islands in the narrowest part of the strait, it would be a long time before we made land with the course we now steered.

As was usual during the whole flight, we conferred with Amundsen, and he thought that there was little probability of finding water clear of ice on the north side of Diomede Islands at that time of the year. That is, it was not Nome we had heard,

1. ELLSWORTH MEASURING ATMOSPHERIC ELECTRICITY.

2. RIISER-LARSEN MAKING AN OBSERVATION DETERMINING POSITION.

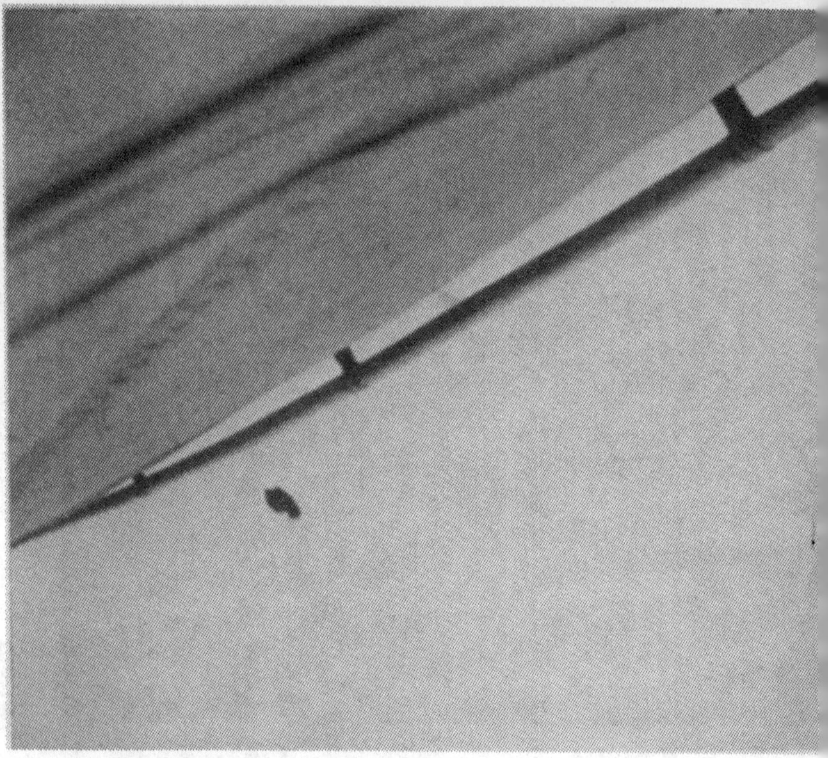

1. AN UNFORGETTABLE MOMENT. THE FLAGS OF NORWAY, AMERICA AND ITALY A[RE] NOW DROPPED ON THE POLE.

2. THE FIRST SIGHT OF LAND AFTER 2,000 MILES—THE COAST OF ALASKA.

and we were probably on the south side of it. We had nothing else to do than to luff up on a course well north-by-east, which, according to our ideas, most quickly would bring us to land. The north-easterly course had this disadvantage: that in the strong wind we proceeded slowly; but it had this compensation: that we had the good fortune to again come in over the ice.

Pieces of ice still occasionally came into the ship, and, should we be compelled to go down, as might happen at any moment, we then had the chances of saving our lives for a time on the ice. The situation on board was not a happy one. Time passed without any indication of land, for sometimes the clouds hung so low that we could see nothing. Nobile's dog, Titina, had somehow got a feeling of the situation, and went backwards and forwards in the gondola, howling and whining, with its tail between its legs. This did not brighten matters.

Hours passed by, and I watched and watched. Then the same thing happened as at Point Barrow—something dark that had the appearance of land loomed up. But what land was it? Was it a place down in Norton Sound, south of Nome, or was it the north side of Kotzebue Sound? The coastline was flat and hidden under a covering of snow, and it was only possible to see for a few hundred meters to each side. And that was the case in spite of the fact that we were moving so low that we lost the aerial weight against the ground. In the distance we could see a hut with Esquimaux outside it. At low altitude and with the least possible speed we steered over and hailed them, but they did not understand us. In the fresh wind we dared not try again. The only thing to do now was to go up through the clouds so as to obtain an observation from the sun, which was then in a favorable position for an observation of the latitude. We then hoped that we should not drift too far before we came down again. When we came up in the sunshine it proved that the sun was so high that an observation could not be taken from the gondola. We tried various courses, but the gondola was always in the shade. There was one way out of it: that I must go up on the top of the airship. Before I came down again Horgen had the calculation ready, so it merely needed putting in the latitude found; for we could therefore at once see on what parallel we were. We were on the north side of Kotzebue Sound. We then proceeded to descend steadily and carefully, but it was some time before we got through the fog, which was more than a thousand meters wide. When we came out of it to a hundred meters altitude we saw only land on all sides.

Well, we had now to steer west so as to come to the sea, but this also took time and was not pleasant. For the most part, it was necessary, in order to be able to see, to go so low that we crept over the ground. At 1.30 Gottwaldt heard the Nome radio-station give its signals, and he succeeded in getting a few bearings from it. These signals, together with a river running east and west, with more twists than any other river in the whole of Alaska, and bearing the suggestive name of the Serpentine River, again gave us the opportunity of determining our exact position. It was then 1.55.

If we could now only keep at this low altitude so as to follow the coast, further navigation would offer no difficulties. I could, therefore, take over the watch for Nobile, so that he could get a necessary rest before we should begin our landing maneuver.

A little later something occurred that proved that it was high time the flight terminated—namely that the amount of work possible without rest or sleep had been exceeded.

We were immediately over the shore-line which goes in the direction north-west east by south-west. There was so strong a storm from the north-west that we had up to 70° drift; that is to say, we had the bow practically dead against the wind, gliding sideways along the shore. We got the stern and port motors at about 80 kilometers air-speed. When the squalls were strong we often stood still above the ground. To leeward astern we had mountains that reached high up into the clouds.

Whilst in this situation the port motor began to

go unevenly. To judge by its conduct during the flight it will be understood that all sorts of things might be expected from it. If it should stop we should, with only one motor working, drift away towards the mountains to leeward. I should eventually have no other resource than to put the bow up through the clouds as quickly as possible in order to attempt to get clear of the mountains. But to go up into the clouds again was the last thing I desired to do. We had had difficulties enough in finding where we were; I therefore gave orders on the telephone for the starboard motor to be set going, so that I might have it in readiness. But it would not work. The port-side motor went so badly that I had to increase the stern-motor to its full 1,400 so as to advance. Such driving for any long period would, however, be a hard demand on it. The time passed, and the starboard motor still remained at a standstill. I subsequently asked Cecioni the reason of this. He himself had been in the starboard gondola at the time, and told me that they had heard the bell and had seen the indicator on the disc move, but they could not grasp the meaning. They could do no more: they were worn out. And no wonder—for these men had worked like heroes, and deserve the highest acknowledgment as a crew. Good, companionable fellows they were, whom their Norwegian ship-mates will always remember with pleasure.

The Navigation Over the Polar Sea

At last the port-side motor recovered, and at 3.30 we rounded Cape Prince of Wales. My work as navigator was at an end. Nobile took over the piloting again, and I set to work to write instructions as to how the assistant parties at Nome should act during the landing. The idea was to throw down the note in a despatch-bag. The members of the crew who were not occupied began to clear up the sleeping-bags and get ready the anchors for landing.

Amundsen has written of the reason for our descending at Teller instead of at Nome. There is little to be said of the actual landing. My efficiency also had come to an end. I was so weary that for a while I commenced to see visions. When we were over Teller and prepared for landing I happily announced to Amundsen that it was an excellent place for landing. "There is plenty of help; I see a whole lot of cavalry down on the shore," for I thought I distinctly saw a number of uniforms and horses. Amundsen took the glasses, and smilingly shook his head. I also took the glasses, but had to rub my eyes before I saw that they were only irregular brown stripes in the sand along the coast!

If the wind had not slackened so suddenly the landing would have been a dramatic story, but now all went well. When the people who had collected rushed forward to the anchor-rope, I called down some orders in Norwegian and continued doing so until Amundsen remarked: "You must speak English here." Then it suddenly occurred to me that after not many hours we had suddenly found ourselves on the opposite side of the globe.

WHY WE CHOSE AN AIRSHIP

When the various difficulties that might be encountered on an expedition like this were taken into consideration, it was quite clear that an airship was preferable to a flying-machine.

With regard to safety the point is this, that an airship floats in the air even if all the motors should fail and there is no necessity to land. If necessary, considerable repairs can in part be effected whilst the airship continues to be driven by the remaining motors. Thus on one occasion one of the cylinders on the starboard motor was dismounted.

Time after time we congratulated ourselves that we were on board an airship and not in a flying-machine.

We had indeed expected to get fog, but not, however, to the extent that we did have it. It lay over 20° latitude, that is to say, for more than 22 kilometers. A man would have to be a rather prejudiced anti-airshipman who would not admit that it is easier and incalculably safer to proceed with an airship in such a fog than with a flying-machine. It may be said that a flying-machine could have kept steadily up over the fog and thereby avoided the formation of ice upon it. That is true enough, but at some time the flying-machine also would have to go down through the belt of fog and it cannot slow off and sink carefully down. It must keep its speed and would run a serious risk of colliding with the side of a mountain.

It must also be asserted that conditions for navigation are much better on an airship than in a flying-machine. There is no shaking and no draught, so that the sun's altitude can be taken as accurately as possible.

As a basis for observation an airship is also much better. We should have observed this had we discovered land and had to chart by photography.

I am convinced that the many who saw our beautiful airship on its flight across Europe have a distinct impression of how safe it appeared.

I will also briefly mention the danger from fire in airships, which so many bring up. Hydrogen-gas is in itself no source of danger, for to burn it must be exposed to the air. That is, a fire must first break out on board so near one of the gas-bags that the covering is burnt right through and the air penetrate, or the gas-bag must be torn to pieces during an accident and the gas combined with air come in contact with open heat before there can be ignition.

The primary source of fire on board an airship is therefore not hydrogen but petrol-gas. Whilst hydrogen combines very easily with air, in such a way that not far from leakage-point there will be over 82% air in it—it is no longer combustible—petrol-gas does not combine with air and is rarefied. In contrast with hydrogen, the specific gravity of which is much less than that of air, petrol-gas is heavier than air and sinks and remains in such places where there is no ventilation. Should there then, from some cause or other, arise a spark or open flame there will be an explosion.

In order to avoid this danger, they are now on the passenger-ships which are being built, constructing motors for raw oil. Although this may not belong to this report, it may nevertheless be interesting perhaps to read why these steps are taken.

When an airship has been flying for a time it has used up a certain amount of petrol. The ship has become lighter and therefore a corresponding amount of gas must be let out so as to descend—something over 1 cubic meter per kilogram of petrol, dependent on the purity of the gas. When it rises again this gas must be replaced if a new weight is to be brought on board. To let out gas in this manner is of course far from economical, and we had the idea that it could be used for working the motor. They set to work attempting to supply the motors with a special gas, a mixture of petrol-gas and hydrogen combined with air. The experiment turned out satisfactorily as it proved that the best mixture was exactly such that it gave about 1 cubic meter of hydrogen per kilogram of petrol. The ship was thus no lighter on its flight, and the petrol consumption went down so strongly that the ship's action was increased by 50% for the same supply of petrol.

Then the possibility of replacing the petrol with raw oil when they also used hydrogen-gas was also considered. These experiments were equally satisfactory. The expenses for hydrogen were lessened to one-seventh of what they were previously. As this arrangement had not been sufficiently tested in practice, we unfortunately could not introduce it. On such an expedition as this the motto must be: "Nothing but the well-tested. No experiments."

Then arose the question as to what type of airship we should choose. As a matter of fact there was no doubt about it, for from the professional journals I had for many years studied Italian airship-building and had been especially interested in N 1, as the price would be affordable even for one of the smaller nations.

It will be recalled that in 1924 we made preparations for an expedition which at the last moment fell through owing to lack of funds. On that occasion I was in Italy and availed myself of a short visit to Rome to inspect the type mentioned, and at the same time made Nobile's acquaintance. I had known his name for a long time from the professional journals and from other sources. I well remember one day out at Ciampino when I admired Nobile's ingenious construction. In the first place it is the many wonderful details of the ship that attract attention. It was these that made me feel proud of being an airshipman. It reminded me of the anecdote, *"Anche io sono pittore."*

Dietrichsen and I were together and we both agreed that we ought to have had such a ship. For our expedition there could be no question of a large ship of the Zeppelin type, for with such a ship an expedition would cost many times over the cost of ours. There could not then have been any expedition before 1927 at the earliest, whilst N 1 was ready and it was merely a question of being able to purchase it. It belonged to the Italian Air Ministry as a military airship.

Thanks to the Italian Government's great interest in our expedition, we succeeded in purchasing the airship at once. But even if we were eager to have the airship we were just as eager to have its constructor, Nobile, with us. We then knew that the preparations, as far as the airship was concerned, were in the best hands. Nobile entered into these preparations with heart and soul and carried out some splendid work. As the most important of these preparations have been dealt with in the Press and should therefore be well known, I will not deal further with them.

The Navigation Over the Polar Sea

The mooring-mast was of especial interest. This method of mooring had never been tried in Italy and was therefore something quite new, although the method has been in use in England and America. As far as quite non-rigid airships were concerned England took it up as early as during the war and in 1921 made the first attempt with such mooring for rigid airships. Major Scott has constructed the English masts and has the credit for the success of this mooring-system. In my opinion it is this system which makes it possible to undertake the enterprise of an airship-route. If one were dependent on the large hangars with the enormous number of people required for bringing the vessel in and out, airship-routes would be far costlier and not suitable for smaller nations. After having finished my theoretic training as an airship-pilot, I then for two months took part in the above-mentioned experiments, but I little thought that the first practical result would be in assisting in the introduction of the system into Italy. Nobile himself in the autumn of last year stayed for a time in England so as to become thoroughly acquainted with the technical side of the matter. As an airshipman I should be very glad if our successful employment of mooring to a mast results in the adoption of this system in Italy and of its being on the whole more widely recognized. Nobile constructed our masts and made a particularly fine job of the masts' tops.

First Crossing of the Polar Sea

The many experiences we had during the expedition of last year were of use this year. This time we knew at once what was required—how much we should have and how the different articles should be arranged.

On the question of clothing I wrote last year: "When flying in the cold it is of great importance that the pilot, who must sit still the whole time, should be warmly or suitably clad. It may be simple enough to find heavy fur-kits which would resist all cold, but it is not so easy to find clothing which is suitable in all respects. Even if we are to sit still, freedom of movement must not be hampered by the dress; this must be light and roomy. What is most important, however, is that it is suitable during the work that comes before the start. There will nearly always be one thing or another to attend to before the start; as far as we were concerned it might be that we should have to land so as to take observations and then start immediately afterwards. If we had such a landing with all our flying-dress on, we should, when we moved about on the ice, soon become heated, the underclothes would become damp and we should most certainly freeze when we once more came into the air. If we had only a rather large outer dress we should, when we took it off, be liable to freeze and that would be no less unfortunate on a start coming just after. Our outer dress consisted therefore of several articles of cloth-ing which, without loss of time, could be taken on or off according to the temperature or according to whether the work was light or strenuous."

It was on the basis of these considerations that the clothing of last year was planned. If we look at the conditions on board an airship, the following points apply not only to the pilot but to the whole crew. We should not land on the way, but there might at any time occur arduous labor and there-fore the same points must be considered, but in a broader sense—as one should not be sitting still on the way. There may be a good deal of climbing to be done on board an airship in places where space is very limited. The dress had therefore to be such that we could move about without being hampered by our coats or getting caught up in anything.

For this reason an overall would be practical, but an overall does not answer the requirement of being easy to throw off; quite the contrary.

In order to suit all purposes we therefore sketched out a dress that looks something like this: trousers, which went up to the chest with braces fastened thereon; a jacket which reached only down to the waist and ended in a belt sewn on; the double-breasted jacket was wide so that there was a double covering for the chest. When we had the dress on it looked like an overall and had all the advantages without the disadvantages of an overall; for if there was work to be done the jacket was discarded easily.

In my experience it is not so necessary to remove the lower portions; it is first and foremost in the upper part of the body one becomes heated.

Then regarding the question of material: it had to be absolutely air-proof, and some good insulating material inside that gave room for much air without the dress being made too wide; the lining was therefore of sheep's wool. But there were also certain points which made it clear that the outer layer should be air-proof—in the literal sense of the word—and not ordinary windproof material. It might happen that we would not reach the coast of Alaska, and might therefore have to make our way on foot. We should then come down in a latitude where we could expect rain and it would be good to be in possession of something water-proof. For this reason we got hold of a special wind-proof material that was also water-proof. As rain would mean a high temperature, we could take off the sheepskin lining and we should have an excellent rainproof dress. The trousers were therefore made long with straps at the bottom so that they could be fastened tightly round the tops of our thick-soled winter boots. The long trousers were not necessary for the flight, as we had procured Russian felt-boots for our feet reaching to the knees (*walinki*). There were also other experiences that were made use of in the shaping of details of the clothing, and so far as I know all were satisfied.

The Navigation Over the Polar Sea

We wore under our flying-dress the same ski-dress as last year—breeches and sweater with hood. As regards this clothing and the tents, we availed ourselves of the experience gained in the last Mount Everest Expedition, and procured from England the same as used on that expedition. Amongst other precautions against cold we had, like last year, filled the compasses and levels, etc., with pure spirit. Even if the oil had not frozen in an oil-level, it still worked too sluggishly in the cold.

The movable parts of the instruments were fitted with a special oil that had been tested at 40° below zero centigrade.

As cooler on the motors we used a 40% glycerine-mixture. Regarding this I will mention a very successful arrangement Nobile had worked out. I mention in another place that we as a rule flew with only two of the three motors, as we obtained the ship's most economic speed of 80 kilometers per hour with 1,200 revolutions on two motors. So as to keep the third motor (as the reserve-motor) warm and ready to start, the boilers on the port and starboard motors were connected up with one another by pipes. The motor that was running then kept the other warm. The pipes ran along the gangways that lead out to the motor-gondolas from the keelson and were well insulated against the cold. This arrangement acted most satisfactorily.

Otherwise as far as the equipment was concerned we were subjected to the same difficulty as last year. Weight had to be spared in every possible way in order that we could take as much petrol as possible.

The skis were made as light as possible and we took only one ski-toboggan with us, whilst most of the crew had light knapsacks.

In the procuring of photographic material we had excellent guidance from our consultant in these matters—Mr. Arvid Odencrantz, lecturer at the Stockholm Technical High School. The photography on the flight was done by Horgen, who had been for a time in Stockholm and who there enlarged his knowledge.

Taught by the bitter experiences of last year we had a plentiful supply of tobacco this time. True enough we could not smoke on board during the flight itself, but we did not know where we might have to land.

The arms supply, etc., was, as mentioned, based on that of the previous year and therefore need not be repeated.

The spare parts for the ship and the motors, as well as tools, were sent to the various landing-places in Europe and at Spitsbergen, according to lists which had been very carefully prepared by the Italian Airship Works under the superintendence of Nobile. It will be illustrative of how complete and well thought out these were when I say that the

"NORGE," PASSING OVER WAINWRIGHT, ALASKA.

AFTER THE FLIGHT—THE "NORGE" DEFLATING.

1. AMUNDSEN AND ELLSWORTH LEAVING TELLER FOR NOME.

2. THE EXPEDITION EN ROUTE FROM NOME TO SEATTLE ON THE S.S. "VICTORIA" AFTER THE FLIGHT.

lists for Oslo, Vadsö, and Svalbard contained respectively about 150, 180, and 450 items.

I am unable to write more about these dry, uninteresting matters. There are so few at any rate who would wish to read about them. I beg the polar travelers of the future who read this book in order to gain information and who do not find all they need, to write to me for further particulars. The address, "Forsvarsdepartementet (Defence Department) Oslo," will always find me. I should perhaps add that so long as we have such a department . . . but I think I shall have left this world before the human race is advanced so far in its development. And when the time comes when you can no longer write to me, then people will no longer go on voyages of discovery in the Arctic regions. Then air routes will proceed on the great impassable circles over the Arctic ice.

SOME FINISHING REMARKS

When we find ourselves on a lecture-tour, with one and often two lectures each day, and struggling to pay the burdensome debt of the expedition, it is not pleasant to sit down at night and write (even if it is with the same object) of spanners and motors, of pemmican and oatmeal-biscuits, of lubricating oils (*à propos,* we used Voltol Oil) and so on. The result is, that the delivery of this my *opus* to the printers has been so delayed that Amundsen has not had the opportunity to "censor" this last part before it goes to print. I will avail myself of the opportunity, for in a few days' time he goes to America and I shall not see him again for a long time, and then any possible wrath on his part will have passed away. I should not like to be in the vicinity if he were angry. It requires much to rouse his temper, and he is not angry without good reason; "but then" the earthquake in San Francisco or the Fall of Pompeii are mere trifles in "clearing the air." He expresses his opinion and then all is well again!

I sit here now in the small hours of the morning and my thoughts go back to the various details of the expedition, of those whom I have undertaken to write. But it is, as I say, a wearisome task. Instead of there cropping up various pleasant episodes—everything passes in review—things also that are not so pleasant persist in presenting themselves.

Instead of forcing my thoughts to concentrate upon that of which I should write, I would prefer to close this account by recording my thoughts.

It was in Rome. In the event of one of the mechanics meeting with an accident we had with us (for training as reserve mechanic) one of our Naval Air Service mechanics, Einar Hansen. One day he came into collision with a tram and was knocked down, but without any serious results. The tram stopped; the people collected. Being one of the most shy men I ever met, he could not bear to be the object of public attention. Unobserved, he crept out between the legs of the onlookers and, running round the tram, took his place amongst the new arrivals to get a sight of the unfortunate man who had been run over!

The delightful recreation on such expeditions is the banter and fun. There are countless stories. The joke was always there, however black the future might appear. Thank God for that. Those who helped most in this, without discriminating too much, were, first and foremost, Gottwaldt and then Malmgren, Ramm, and Gustav Amundsen. Of the Italians it is difficult to pick out a single one, but perhaps it might be Caratti.

À propos Caratti. It was dangerous to be a bird in those parts of Alaska where he happened to be. Caratti could spend the whole day in dismantling the airship, which he and his comrades had to attend to, but when the evening came he took a gun on his shoulder and set off after "papagalli." Should "papagalli" indicate what he brought back with him in the early hours of the morning, then it must include everything that flaps about with wings. If he had the misfortune to wound a bird he would wade out into the ice-cold water, right up over his mouth so that he panted for air, in order to spare the bird needless suffering.

Pomella was fair-haired, quiet, and gentle. He

belonged to the stern motor-gondola, and kept it going steadily and evenly without jarring, all the way from Rome to Teller.

Then there was the ever-smiling and polite Arduino, blue-eyed and Nordic. And the circus-artiste, our rigger Alesandrini; with slight exaggeration I declare that he could hang on by his eyelashes and work with feet and hands on each side of him. At one moment he was on the top of the ship to see that the gas-valves were closed fast again after use, the next moment he would be down amongst us in the pilot-gondola to see if he could help us. He was always smiling.

But above them all was the chief, Cecioni. On account of his comprehensive knowledge and experience of airships, as well as for his gray hair and *embonpoint*, he might have been my father, and yet he was not much older than I. When he sat down at the end of the table it was like looking at the Apennines themselves—and his words were just as weighty!

We of the other three nations were all fond of these good, likeable fellows. I have said this before and repeat it: we shall always remember them as the capital fellows they were, and we would gladly go out with them again.

When Nobile comes into my thoughts at the close it is because—and rightly—I have mentioned his name so often before. He is of that quiet, contained type whose brain is always at work on something of serious interest. He therefore rarely smiles, and so one accepts it as a benefaction when he does. There was nothing that afforded us a greater sense of security than to know that the ship's constructor was on board. If anything might happen to the vessel there was no one who would be more aware of it or know the right steps to take than he.

One by one they appear before me now when the whole personnel is reviewed. We have Malmgren there, the Swedish member of the expedition, and without a doubt its most popular one. For three long years he had lain up there with the *Maud*. It was clear therefore that he was the best meteorologist procurable. It would have been natural for him to have thought a little of himself and to have preferred to go for a good holiday after such a long tour, but Malmgren is not that type. He immediately went ahead with heart and soul in making the necessary preparations to join us. He was not a fellow-countryman of Bellman for nothing and was always ready for a joke. If it is true that a good laugh lengthens life, then, thanks to Malmgren, I shall live to a ripe old age. I tell in my lecture of his various nicknames on the voyage: Uncle Poodle, Royal North-blast, and the Swedish Imp. The meteorologist is the closest coöperator of the navigator and a better I have never met. In years to come, I shall look forward to each day I have the opportunity of meeting him.

Then I see Ellsworth. Had he been the most ordinary mortal, I would have been moved when he said: "I am so awfully fond of Norway." And when it actually is Ellsworth who says it . . .

In my German school-book there was a story of a son who stood beside his mother's grave, and who thought: "How can a mother's love be closed up in this narrow mold?" Often have I thought similarly when I have been with Ellsworth. A great heart and a wonderful smile sums the man up. Through his admiration for Amundsen the expeditions of 1925 and 1926 were accomplished. Without him they could never have been possible. When I think of you, Ellsworth, I still see the glance in your eye and hear the tone of your voice when you answer Amundsen: "Yes, Captain."

Then come the Norwegians. The best men you could think of—and what a selection! If we had accepted all who offered themselves we could have sent off an airship every day for a long time. They did not ask for wage, or remuneration or life-insurance. *Was schert mich Weib, was schert mich Kind, ich trage weit besseres Verlangen.* They gave themselves to their country.

Wisting, Gottwaldt, Horgen, Ramm, Gustav Amundsen, Storm-Johnsen, and, last but not least, Omdal. With such men, and such chiefs as Amundsen and Ellsworth, it is indeed easy to be second-in-command.

And so these two expeditions that form a whole, the Svalbard—Pole—Alaska exploration, are over. These two years were strenuous. But that which asserts itself through all is the joy of having worked under Amundsen.

He is not the type of leader who uses his subordinates as orderlies. He chooses out each man for each single task and leaves it to him to fill his position according to his own initiative. Then Amundsen moves round and sees that all is going as it should. So long as this is so he says nothing, and some perhaps do not notice he is there. But when difficulties begin to appear, then his presence is felt— a wonderful feeling of security. Each man does his best at his post. Should anything go wrong then we know Amundsen will be able to pull us through.

Well did I understand Wisting when we once chatted of these things and he said: "If we were in want of food and he said one must sacrifice himself for the others, I would gladly go quietly out into the snowdrift and die."

That says everything; and I must close. But I should like to record, and, pretentious as it may seem, preserve for those who come after, the finest incident I have ever seen. It was a perfect July day when, after the expedition, we came home to Oslo. Amundsen stood there to respond to the speeches of welcome. He happened to have under his arm the flag which had flown from the airship during the whole of the voyage. It had been entrusted to him by the King and Queen, and was to be given back to them that day. Amundsen said:

"There are so many who have asked me what it was that has always spurred me on these journeys." He took the flag, unfolded it, and held it up before the crowd: "This. This has always spurred me on."

Roald! You yourself were moved when you uttered those words, and you brought tears to your comrades' eyes also. We who had had the good fortune to learn to know you by having labored under you, we knew that this most noble of all sentiments, love of country, was not an empty phrase in your mouth—it was no figure of speech such as men use on festal occasions or when they are moved by strong feeling. For you this sentiment has been the foundation of your whole life. By this your every thought is fostered: How can I best serve my country?

The North-West Passage, the South Pole, the North-East Passage, Svalbard—North Pole—Alaska.

This perhaps is my swan-song as a writer—so little do we know—but I cannot add a better conclusion than this:

Thank you, thank you from us all, Roald.

FINN MALMGREN

CHAPTER ELEVEN

*Weather and Weather Warnings
During the Polar Flight*

CHAPTER XI

WEATHER AND WEATHER WARNINGS DURING THE POLAR FLIGHT

Whoever follows the description of the voyage of the *Norge* from Italy to Alaska cannot help but notice how almost all the difficulties encountered by the airship were connected with unfortunate conditions of weather. For the voyage through the air to be accomplished with a happy result it had to take place under certain very favorable meteorological conditions. On every occasion when these were more or less unfavorable the difficulties also commenced. Still, on the other hand, the story of the expedition shows that on the whole the various stages of the journey were favored with the best of weather. That such was the case was not a matter of mere chance. With the help of a well-planned organization and a good deal of labor we succeeded, as a matter of fact, in making a start at such points of time when the weather *was* fine. Before referring to our telegraphic organization and the work of the meteorologist on board, we will first see by what dangers the *Norge* was threatened on the part of the weather, and how the various meteorological elements can play a part in the case of flying by airship.

[251]

First Crossing of the Polar Sea

That element, which is of the greatest importance in flying is the *wind*. In the use of airships the wind is an important factor, not only during the flight itself, but also for the start and the landing. When it blows there is then danger in taking the airship out of the hangar, or, after the flight, in bringing her in again. There is the risk that the wind will take hold of the ship, which, with her great volume exposed to the wind, is an appreciable object of attack, and will thrust her against one of the frames in the opening of the hangar. Such handling cannot be endured by any airship because, with her fragile steel construction, she cannot in any case worthy of mention resist such pressure. The danger is, of course, the greatest when the wind blows straight in from the side as the ship passes the door or when the wind is squally. In such cases it requires an average force of wind of only about four or five meters per second to make. Such maneuvers in and out are extremely risky. This effect of the wind in starting or landing is often very troublesome. During the voyage from Rome to Teller it occurred no less than three times that a too strong wind at the starting-place itself prevented us from drawing the *Norge* out of the hangar. The start was thus rendered impossible in spite of the fact that meteorological conditions in other respects appeared to be favorable.

Attempts were made to reduce the difficulties in

the start and in the landing by the use of landing-masts. These masts allow of starting or landing maneuvers also with a relatively high force of wind, and also make one quite independent of the direction of the wind on the flying-ground. On the journey to Alaska there were masts at Oslo and King's Bay.

It is not, however, only before or after the flight that an airship is dependent on the wind. The airship has not the same great speed as the modern aeroplane; the normal speed of the *Norge,* for instance, was only 80 kilometers an hour. It is self-evident that with such a rate of speed through the air the rate over the ground against even a moderate headwind is considerably reduced. A strong side-wind is also unfavorable, as it causes a strong drifting out of the course, and this obliges the pilot to steer up against the wind, whereby the rate of speed over the ground is always lessened. On the other hand, a fair wind is naturally advantageous, as it decreases the time of flight. A strong fair wind, may, however, be dangerous, as is the case with all strong winds. This is due to the fact that a strong wind, as a rule, is accompanied by eddies and other disturbances in the ocean of the air, and this results in the different parts of the airship being acted upon by the air with different speeds and directions. This causes serious strains, which at worst can break the ship in two. Such air-eddies we met with during our voyage north of Leningrad, when we flew over the tongue of land that separates the large lakes, Ladoga and Onega, from each other. In this case they were probably caused by the inequalities in temperature and conditions of friction which are found between the ice on the lakes and the land lying between them.

It is, however, not the wind alone that may be dangerous for an airship. In the colder regions there are also certain forms of precipitation that may be troublesome enough. All kinds of precipitation are, moreover, unfavorable, as they reduce the range of vision, and, in this way, make navigation difficult. The situation becomes directly dangerous when the precipitation settles on the ship in a frozen condition, or when she is in other ways exposed to being iced over. Wet snow and sub-chilled rain are examples of obstructive precipitations. Of these the chilled rain is the more dangerous, as the rain-drops may freeze when they touch the airship, and become a compact layer of smooth ice. A coating similar to this is formed also when flying through fog consisting of chilled rain-drops. This phenomenon of ice-coatings occurs principally in temperatures just under freezing-point. At lower temperatures the danger is less, but should the temperature go down towards 15° below freezing-point, there is a risk of a rime-frost coating on the balloon, especially when proceeding through fog or hazy weather. At such low temperature the rime-frost, however, is comparatively light, and, besides, is so crisp that for the most part it blows away in the draught of the air. The danger from ice-coating is this—that the balloon may in a short time become too heavy. A coating of so much as one millimeter over the whole of the surface of the *Norge* would increase her weight by several tons. The ice, however, does not settle evenly over the whole surface of the ship, but chiefly on those parts that are most exposed to the wind—that is, on the front part of the bow. This causes the ship to lose her original balance and to become too heavy in the bow.

If this settlement of ice has begun, the danger is so great, in fact, that the pilot, by every means in his power, must endeavor to come out of that region of air where the coating of ice can form. This can sometimes be done by choosing another altitude of flight. He may often, for instance, by steering upwards, rise above the chilled fog. In other cases it may answer well to attempt another route towards his goal. This is especially to be recommended if there is a choice offered between a route that goes over the land and another that proceeds over the sea. When one is exposed to ice-coating on one of these routes, it is often possible that the danger may be avoided on the other. If no way of escape is seen from the region of ice-coating, and it be possible to reverse, this ought to be done. If one has a fair wind and the goal is near, an attempt may be made at stopping the motors and drifting with the wind. In this case the formation of ice in a high degree diminishes, especially if it be caused by fog in hazy weather.

Above we have mentioned the influence that wind and precipitation have upon an airship. We will now, in a few words, touch upon one more meteorological element that is of the greatest importance for the aviator, namely, range of vision. There must be good visibility. Fog is a serious obstacle for the navigator, as it prevents him from seeing the ground, and from thereby effecting the necessary drift-calculations. The fog, moreover, renders a landing impossible, even if one can reach the landing-place. On an aeronautic voyage of discovery, where the object is research in new regions, the fog naturally presents special difficulties. Thus a thick fog might have easily doomed the whole purpose of our journey from Svalbard to Alaska to failure. In laying the plans for the flying expedition, the greatest attention was also given to the fog, the flight being fixed for a point of time when the probability of fog was as slight as possible. In the Polar Sea the months of June, July and August are the most prolific in fogs. The whole sea is, during these months, covered with drifting ice, whose temperature may rise above the freezing-point. This causes the surface of the sea to seek to chill the

Weather and Weather Warnings

masses of air that drift from a warmer region in over the polar cap. In the chilling that these masses of air undergo, a good deal of their moisture is deposited as fog. In spring, on the contrary, there is practically no fog, as a similar chilling on the surface of the sea does not then occur. Earlier in the year the cold and the conditions of light make a long flight impossible, and as early as in May the fog begins to appear. The flight from Svalbard to Alaska was therefore fixed for the close of April, but difficulties in the erection of hangar and mast at King's Bay delayed the start. On the flight over the Pole we met fog, although not to such an extent that it threatened our research in the unknown regions. We have now seen how fateful the weather in many cases may become in flying with an airship. It was, therefore, necessary to arrange the flight from Rome to Alaska in such a way that the meteorological conditions in each stage of the voyage were as favorable as possible. The leaders must, therefore, have opportunity to acquire reliable advice regarding the best time for starting for each distance. Subsequently, during the voyage itself, they must, moreover, be supplied with all the meteorological advice and information that were needful.

The honor of having arranged the whole of the meteorological precautionary service belongs to the head of the Norwegian Meteorological Institute, Director Th. Hesselberg. Director Hesselberg could, thanks to his international connections, procure help for the expedition from several central institutes abroad—from the Italian, French, English, Swedish, Russian, and American. The greatest assistance, however, that the expedition obtained was from the Norwegian Institute. It was thus made possible for the meteorologist of the expedition to study for several months the Norwegian weather report at the Weather Office in Bergen, and he thereby got the opportunity of becoming better acquainted with the new weather-report methods which have been in the first place worked out by the meteorologists J. Bjerknes, Solberg, and Bergeron. The expedition, moreover, had the loan from the Institute of all meteorological instruments that are required for taking the usual observations. During the flight itself the Institute assisted further by observations and warnings which were sent out by weather-warning centers in Oslo and Tromsö. This point we shall revert to later on.

The meteorological advice that is required so that the expedition may be successfully carried out falls, as mentioned before, into two divisions—services before the start and work during the flight itself. As far as the former is concerned the intention, then, was this: that the start at each new place should be fixed upon in coöperation between the meteorologists of the expedition and the local institute. Through the ready kindness of various authorities, the meteorologist of the expedition had the opportunity to analyze the state of the day's weather at the institute of the place, whereby it became possible to get an independent comprehension of the conditions. The expedition, however, had its own meteorological station also in Rome and at King's Bay before the start.

During the flight the *Norge* had its own meteorologist on board. His duty was to foresee the weather, and, in conjunction therewith, give the leaders advice in those matters where the weather more or less plays a part. It was thus his work to point out, by the help of synoptic charts, the best flying route, and, by the help of telegraphed pilot-balloon pointers, indicate the best altitude of flight. Besides this he should give the probable value of a number of meteorological factors in landing, as, for instance, the barometric position of the place, and its temperature in cases when these were not telegraphed. Finally, he should take the observations of weather that were collected during the *Norge's* voyage. These included, amongst others, barometer, thermometer, and humidity readings, and also observations above the clouds and such things. During the polar flight itself there were added a number of air-electric measurements.

In order to enable weather reports to be worked out on board it was necessary that the meteorologist on the *Norge* should have access to the same telegram-material as was used by all other weather officers in Europe. This material, which was picked up by the radio-telegraphist on board, contains observations taken several times daily from most European countries, as well as from several ships in the Atlantic and Mediterranean. Beside these ordinary telegrams the *Norge* received certain special reports which were sent out exclusively for our sake. These mostly contained observations from places on our way, but occasionally also shorter warnings for the weather in the immediate future. The telegraphist on the *Norge* often succeeded during the flight in coming into direct correspondence with one or other institute, to which we then could direct enquiries regarding what was of interest to us. The organization of the meteorological labors is best illustrated by a brief description of the sources of assistance that were at the disposal of the meteorologist during the various stages of the journey from Rome to Teller.

The start from Italy on the voyage from Rome to Pulham took place after coöperation with the weather-report center in Rome and its head, Professor F. Eredia. Before the start we received a telegram from France in which the point of time for the departure was indicated as not very favorable. Nor did we, either, regard the situation as being quite ideal; but, as in all probability it would come to be still worse in the next few days, we thought, however, that the start ought to be made. During the flight we received several special telegrams from France and England, which were very valuable, especially when we came into difficulties during the later part of the journey. In North France, indeed, the airship was caught by a strong cyclone, which approached rapidly from the south. We got a hard north-easterly wind, which to a high degree lessened our speed. By forcing all the three motors on the *Norge* we succeeded, however, in flying from the cyclone, so that we could subsequently land under ideal conditions in England.

The landing took place at Pulham. Here the English Meteorological Institute had established a special weather-report department for our sake. This was directed by Mr. Giblett, one of England's best "weather-prophets." The prominent Norwegian meteorologist also, Dr. J. Bjerknes, who for some time had stayed in England, went to Pulham. Both these scientists assisted the expedition in continuing the flight, after a day or two, to Oslo.

The start was made under promising conditions of wind, but over the North Sea we met with fog. The weather cleared, however, under the Norwegian coast, and there was good visibility when, after a speedy voyage, we landed at Oslo. On the way we got into communication with the Norwegian Meteorological Institute, which every hour sent reports from the landing-place. Immediately after arrival the meteorologist of the *Norge* visited the weather-warning center in Oslo, and the result of the visit was that the *Norge* that very same day continued her voyage to Leningrad. The meteorologist considered it to be risky to remain long in Oslo, as a storm-center was approaching from the west.

The voyage from Oslo to Leningrad was marked by fog. The fog stretched over the whole of Sweden, and continued out over the Baltic. It did not begin to lighten before the mouth of the Gulf of Finland was reached. A so protracted fog naturally made navigation difficult to a great extent, and it was not until after considerable trouble that we could land at the flying-ground at Gatchina, a small suburb of Leningrad. In Leningrad the expedition obtained all the assistance imaginable from the Meteorological Central Institute, which, be it remarked in passing, proved to be an institution of model organization. Through its mediation we obtained the promise of extra telegrams during the continuation of our voyage. These telegrams proved to be extremely valuable during the coming flight, Leningrad—Vadsö—King's Bay.

The last-mentioned part of the polar flight is regarded by many as being the most dangerous of the whole voyage. There can also be found many reasons for this part being considered risky. The sea between North Norway and Svalbard is one of the most stormy in the world, and in spring there is great risk of fog and the formation of ice-coating. Moreover, the distance is very long. On this stretch the airship must have, to enable her to start and to go down, quiet or almost quiet weather in three places: Leningrad, Vadsö, and King's Bay. Besides, there must at least be good visibility in the vicinity of the landing-places. Now it is no easy task to prophesy the weather for so long a time as two long days ahead, such as now must be done in Leningrad. It is especially difficult to foresee the weather in the most northerly part of Europe, where the telegraph-stations lie far apart, and there are seldom found any vessels on the seas that send out observations.

However, the expedition received good assistance. Besides getting help from the Russians, we also had daily advice regarding the possibility of a start from the meteorological center at Tromsö—that institute which is perhaps best aware of conditions in the Arctic Ocean. These telegrams, unfortunately, often arrived a trifle too late to Leningrad; but the telegram that reached us on the night before our departure was, however, extremely welcome, as it confirmed the accuracy of the start already determined upon.

The voyage northwards from Leningrad proceeded against a contrary wind, but otherwise under favorable conditions. As we began to approach North Norway we got, besides the usual dispatches, special telegrams also every hour. These contained observations from the northern part of Norway, Svalbard, and two small islands in the Norwegian sea, Jan Mayen and Björnöen. By this means every unpleasant surprise on the part of the weather was rendered out of the question, and we could have turned in good time if conditions in the Arctic had been too unfavorable.

All went well to Vadsö, and we were here some hours in order to take in petrol and gas. On the way between Vadsö and Svalbard the weather was worse, with much fog whilst we passed Björnöen. Later, when the *Norge* came to the coast of Svalbard, we also met with heavy snow-squalls. At the same time a telegram came from King's Bay reporting that there was thick drifting snow. The situation appeared threatening, but, as the synoptic charts showed that the snow could scarcely be falling other than in squalls, we continued, as we reckoned upon practicable visibility in between the falls of snow. On landing at King's Bay the range of vision was also good. On this voyage we noticed with satisfaction that ordinary snow did not attach itself to the balloon, but was at once swept away by the strong draught. Wet snow is probably more dangerous, but we did not meet with such during the whole of our flight.

At King's Bay we established our own "weather office," which had the advantage the whole time of a

Weather and Weather Warnings

close coöperation with the institute in Tromsö.
The necessary telegrams were passed on partly by
the King's Bay radio, and partly by the Norwegian
naval vessel *Heimdal,* which had been sent up to
Svalbard exclusively for our sake.

As it was necessary to find good weather conditions at King's Bay for the polar flight, we had also
to give attention to the *Norge's* carrying capacity,
which must be as great as possible so that the airship should be able to carry all the necessities for
the last tour. The carrying capacity depends in no
small degree on the temperature and state of the
barometer. The temperature must be low and the
air-pressure high, for with the fall of every degree
in the temperature, and with the increase of every
millimeter in the air-pressure, we gained respectively 70 and 30 kilograms in carrying capacity.
The most important conditions for a successful
flight were, however, now, as previously, favorable
wind and good visibility.

We had to wait several days at King's Bay before
we could think of continuing. The reason was that
one of the motors had become useless, and had to be
exchanged for another. During this time our little
institute worked intensely. Three synoptic charts,
based on observations taken at 7, 13, and 18 Greenwich Mean Time, were taken each day. Moreover,
pilot-balloons were sent up several times daily by an
Italian aerologist, a brother of Nobile. By the help

of these balloons the direction and force of the wind in the upper strata of air were ascertained.

During our time of waiting the weather was ideal for a polar flight, and this Commander Byrd could assure us of. On one of these days, indeed, Byrd accomplished his famous North Pole journey, and on his return reported brilliant sunshine and slight winds.

Little by little the time approached when we ourselves could think of flying. On the 10th of May, in the evening, it was announced that the airship was now ready. We now merely waited for word from the meteorologists.

The synoptic chart of the evening appeared favorable. A great high-pressure area extended from Nova Zembla, over the Pole, right into Canada. Such a barometric maximum was exactly what we had hoped for. It promised comparatively cold weather, with clear sky, and variable slight winds over the polar cap. According to the charts, Svalbard was on the west side of the high-pressure area. This indicated a probable fair wind up towards the Pole. The only unfavorable message came from Point Barrow, on the north coast of Alaska, and reported fog out along the coast. We hoped that this fog would disappear before we came there, and decided to start. The weather-warning center at Tromsö and the meteorologist of the expedition were agreed that the time for starting was favorable. The start was fixed to take place at 10 o'clock of the night between the 10th and the 11th of May.

Whilst these pleasant plans were being made it began to blow at King's Bay. The wind increased as the evening came on, and at 11 o'clock it was clear that the old enemies of the expedition—local winds round the hangar—would make departure impossible. The wind perhaps did not blow so very hard, but it was squally, as it so often is in narrow fjords with mountains on both sides. Under such conditions it was considered risky to draw the ship out of the hangar. Most of the members of the expedition were therefore sent to bed, with instructions that they should be wakened later in the night if the wind calmed down. The rest remained at the hangar in order to watch the weather.

It was a long watch to keep. Twice the wind slackened away so much that a messenger was sent to arouse the sleepers, but scarcely had he gone on his way before the wind began again and the awakening had to be postponed. Not until 6 A.M. did it become so quiet that they could all be awakened and preparations for the start begun.

In the course of the night the meteorological situation had become worse; the barometer on Jan Mayen began to fall. This indicated an approaching cyclone which perhaps might be dangerous for the high-pressure over Svalbard. We had, therefore, so much the greater reason to attempt to avail ourselves of the slackening of the wind, which occurred towards morning. If we did not get away now it might be weeks before we again found an available opportunity. Captain Amundsen therefore decided to bring out the airship, in spite of the wind having increased somewhat during the preparations.

This proceeding took place at 8.30 A.M. Greenwich Mean Time (G.M.T. is also used in what follows). It was an exciting moment when the airship slowly glided out of the hangar, but all went well, and after a few minutes the *Norge* found herself in brilliant sunshine on the flat outside the hangar. Some minutes later—8.55 A.M.—the start took place.

Before we begin a description of the last part of the flight it is perhaps advantageous to recount the precautions that were taken so as to secure the *Norge* against surprises from the weather. In the winter of 1925-6 we had worked to get into operation an arrangement which made it possible for the *Norge* during the whole polar flight to obtain reliable meteorological announcements from the northern parts of Europe, Asia, and America. In the first place, it was necessary to procure the required observations. In Europe this was not difficult, as we have several good stations that lie far towards the north. The various countries thus send out by radio regular observations from Iceland, Svalbard,

Weather and Weather Warnings

Jan Mayen, Björnöen, Nova Zembla, Waigatsch, the mainland of Norway and North Russia, Sweden, Finland, and the North Atlantic Ocean. As far as Asia is concerned, the Russian report contains observations from Jakutsk and places on the Trans-Siberian railway. Through the kindness of the Soviet authorities the transmission was completed with meteorological telegrams from a little place on the Bering Sea, Anadyn, and hereby this despatch could be regarded as being satisfactory. The conditions in America were the worst. The observations that were sent out from there by radio contained merely a few and delayed reports from Alaska and Canada, the most important regions as far as we were concerned. On application to the Weather Bureau in Washington, Director Hesselberg, however, succeeded in bringing it about that the usual reports were increased with observations from the most northerly part of the continent. Moreover, we got the promise of a special daily report from Cordova containing observations from five different places in Alaska—St. Paul, Nome, Eagle, Cordova, and Kodiak.

After we had succeeded in getting the necessary observations, the next problem was how these could be communicated to the *Norge's* meteorologist in the surest way. An ordinary meteorological institute obtains the great majority of its observations by listening to the wireless stations of various nations in turn and at fixed times. Now it was not, however, probable that the *Norge* during the polar flight would be able to hear these wireless centers, as the distances to them were too great. There was found, then, only one way out of the difficulty, namely to collect the radio telegrams of the different countries at one place and then forward them to the *Norge* over a single large radio station powerful enough to be heard over the whole Polar Sea. Such a powerful station was found in west Norway—Stavanger radio. An application to the Norwegian Telegraph authorities requesting to have the use of this radio station to transfer the meteorological telegrams to the *Norge* was met with obliging acquiescence, and the result was that the Telegraph directions placed this station gratis at the disposal of the expedition.

Stavanger radio was to send its telegrams at the following hours: 6.10, 8.30, 11.20, 14.40, 17.20, 20.00 and 21.20. As will be noticed, there is an interval in the telegraph hours of the night, so that the telegraphist on the *Norge* might be able to obtain a little rest. The telegrams were to contain all the necessary observations with the exception of the Cordova report. This, which could not be received in Norway, we hoped to be able to hear direct when the airship approached America.

The observations reaching the *Norge* were to be entered on the synoptic charts, of which the meteorologist should draw three each day. By the help of these charts he could then foretell the weather. There should also be placed on the chart the observations which might be effected from the airship itself.

After this explanation of how we had thought the meteorological work would be able to be arranged during the polar flight, we will now return to King's Bay, where the airship has risen above the snow-covered ground.

The start took place, as mentioned before, on the 11th of May at 8.55 A.M. The temperature was 8° below zero, centigrade, and the air-pressure was 771 millimeters. On the land a slight east-south-east-breeze was blowing, which at an altitude of a couple of hundred meters was transformed to a somewhat stronger south-easterly breeze. After half an hour only the wind became still, and this lasted until 11 A.M., when it again began to blow from the south and the south-east. These favorable winds prevailed until about 7 P.M., when they were succeeded by a slight north-easterly breeze. This slackened soon, so that there was complete absence of wind at 10 P.M.

The boundary line in the Polar Sea between the open water and the drift-ice was passed after two hour's flight. After that we saw open water only on rare occasions in a passage through the ice. The temperature at the altitude of flight sank steadily from 5° below freezing-point over King's Bay to to 12° below zero on 88° latitude on the European side. From this place it began to rise slowly. For more than eleven hours we flew in brilliant sunshine. On 87° latitude we met with fog, which, however, soon disappeared. Between 88° and 89° latitude we came into a new belt of fog. The fog lay, however, so low that we could fly over it by rising to 7,000 meters altitude.

At the Pole itself the fog thinned. The weather, as if for the occasion, at this longed-for spot on the earth's surface, can be described in a few words. The sky for the most part was covered with stratocumulus and altocumulus clouds. There was complete cessation of wind. The temperature at about 300 meters' altitude was 2° below zero, and the barometer, sea-level, about 775 millimeters. The atmosphere was hazy, but cleared soon after.

From the Pole we set our course towards Point Barrow. The journey from the Pole was, at the beginning, favored with good visibility, but between 86° and 85° latitude we met with continuous fog. The fog and snowfall prevailed fairly unbroken afterwards on the way down to Teller. The fog was fortunately not so thick that it prevented us from seeing the land below us. On the other hand, it caused, at certain times, rime frost on the balloon, and this was perhaps what we feared most of all. The formation of ice on the balloon is, as mentioned

THE FIRST AMERICAN FLAG TO CROSS THE POLAR SEA.

before, extremely dangerous. It was probably such
that caused the first flying disaster in the Polar Sea,
when the pioneer Andrée and both his brave companions met their fate.

The rime frost occurred for the first time on 85°
30'. In a short time it covered all those parts of the
balloon that were exposed to strong wind. It chiefly
settled on the projecting metal-parts of the airship,
on instruments, etc., but it also attached itself to the
wooden propellers and the rope work. The smallest
layer came on the balloon covering itself; this was
due possibly to its being warmed from the gas,
which probably had a somewhat higher temperature
than the surrounding air.

As soon as the rime frost began, precautions were
taken to come as quickly as possible away from the
ice-formation zone. The first maneuver consisted
in increasing the altitude of flight to about 800
meters in order to rise above the fog-belt. This
failed. The fog was perhaps a little lighter at a
greater altitude, but the clogging of ice proved more
quickly greater. We attempted then to sink as low
down as possible, and continue the flight only a
couple of hundred meters above the ice. This was
better. The meteorologist, who carefully observed
the ice-formation at the various levels, could now
state that the clogging had become quite inconsiderable. The cause of this was that the temperature in the layer of air nearest the ice was from

3-4° lower than that higher up, and, as mentioned before, the danger from ice-coating is less at lower temperatures. After the flight had proceeded for an hour at this altitude the formation of rime frost, however, again increased, and we had once more to try another altitude. This time—it was about on 83° latitude—we succeeded in rising over the fog, and, although we still observed a slight formation of rime frost, this was, however, no more dangerous than that we could regard ourselves as rescued. On the whole stretch down to 74° latitude we flew over fog, in which, however, many breaks were found. The sky above us was free of clouds. The wind was, on the whole, favorable from the Pole and down to 80°, but later we met with quite a strong breeze from the south-east, which decreased our speed.

On 74° latitude we came into fog, which it was no longer possible to fly over. The formation of rime frost recommenced, and this time stronger than before. After half an hour we came out of the danger-zone, but got instead a good deal of snow. Later during the flight we came, on several occasions, upon new ice-settlements. By steadily observing how much ice clogged, and, according to these observations searching for the most favorable altitude for flight, we succeeded, however, in avoiding a catastrophe, which otherwise was imminent. That the danger from ice-coating was really threatening is best proved by the fact that on landing, the ice which had settled on the balloon weighed one ton. This settled principally on the front part of the airship, and would without doubt have made the ship unbalanced if we had not compensated for its weight by using more petrol on the flight from the front tanks than from the back ones.

It was, however, not only ice-coating that caused us trouble during the latter part of the polar flight. We also had another misfortune come upon us which perhaps disturbed us just as much—our wireless station ceased to act. This occurred whilst we still found ourselves far from the coast of Alaska, and the cause was partly atmospheric electric disturbances and partly formation of ice on the aerial. This produced a stoppage in the receiving of meteorological telegrams.

The weather-forecasting on board had previously been performed according to the prearranged plan. Stavanger radio had, at the times arranged upon beforehand, sent the necessary observations which the meteorologist on board entered on his chart. As we approached the coast we required, however, charts according to the very latest reports, in order to decide upon the most favorable landing-place and the best way to it. And it was these charts that we could not get.

As was natural, we wished to land as far south as possible. Even at the beginning of the voyage it had been resolved that the *Norge,* if the weather permitted, should continue her flight quite down to Nome, a little town on the south side of Seward Peninsula. The last synoptic chart, which, when we reached the north coast of Alaska, was more than twenty-four hours old, showed a cyclone that two days later was expected to lie with its center at one place or another in Alaska Bay. According to this calculation, Nome should be a favorable landing-place, as the wind probably became northerly along the west coast of Alaska. This would bring fair wind on the way down, and, as Nome lies protected against northerly winds, it meant also that the conditions of wind during landing would be favorable. The leaders also then decided that we should try to go forward to Nome or some other place on the south coast of Seward Peninsula.

At 7.25 of the morning of the 13th of May we got our landfall just in the vicinity of Point Barrow. The wind had little by little gone from light southeast breeze to very fresh west-south-west, and the atmosphere was extremely hazy. Now and then we had a passing fall of snow. The temperature was 2° below zero.

After having followed the coast towards the south-west for some hours, we flew over the peninsula that lies north of Kotzebue Sound and farther towards Bering Strait. The wind by degrees turned to north-westerly and increased to a gale, which occasionally went up to 18 meters per second (strong gale). The airship proved extremely capable of resistance, in spite of the fact that the strain must have been very heavy in that exceedingly turbulent air. The barograph-curve shows that the airship was cast over 100 meters up and down by the gusts of wind in fractions of a minute. If one stood in the keelson at one end of the ship and looked towards the other end, one could observe how the whole steel skeleton of the ship bent before the gusts of wind. The situation was so serious that the leaders decided that the ship should make in to the nearest land, so much the more as we now observed rime frost. We therefore flew in over Kotzebue Sound until we got land in sight on the north side of the bay. After having taken our bearings we again flew out, following the coast in a westerly direction. The gale raged continuously, but decreased somewhat after we rounded Cape Prince of Wales—the west point of Seward Peninsula. The wind was, however, continuing very squally so that the airship steered badly.

The conditions for landing did not appear very promising; and besides, it was blowing too hard. The only thing we could hope for was that the wind down by the ground would be considerably weaker, and this probably was the case, as the strip of coast, as was expected, lay in the lee of a high mountain. The visibility, fortunately, had become better in the last few hours, and no longer placed hindrances in the way of navigation.

The airship had now been in the air for seventy hours, and all longed to descend. When we therefore discovered a small lagoon on the coast that seemed to offer a favorable landing-place, the leaders gave up the idea of proceeding to Nome, and decided to land on the lagoon. On its shore there lay a small town, which is called Teller, and it was determined to go down as near this town as possible.

The landing took place at 8 A.M. on the 14th of May. It proceeded very favorably, which to a great extent was due to the fact that the expedition was lucky with conditions of wind. As a matter of fact, the north-wester very considerably decreased a little before the landing; only afterwards, when the airship had been moored, did it blow up again with renewed force. The same rate of the wind force was found again in the registering from Nome, 120 kilometers from there, though the force of the winds in Teller was altogether higher. Nome registered the following average wind force per hour: 6-7 A.M.: 5.3 m/sec.; 7-8 A.M.: 3.1 m/sec.; 8-9 A.M.: 2.2 m/sec.; 9-10 A.M.: 3.6 m/sec.; and 10-11 A.M.: 5.8 m/sec. The weather on landing, moreover, may be described in a few words. The temperature was 2° above zero. The sky was covered with rainclouds (nimbus), which, however, for the moment had not given any downpour. The visibility was good, in contrast to the conditions at Nome, where at the same time they had fog. This shows that the landing at Teller, from a meteorological point of view, was in a high degree to be preferred to a possible landing at Nome. Even if this had not proved quite impracticable, it must, however, have offered great difficulties.

The author of this article has, on the other hand, asked himself if we could not have avoided many of the dangers that we met with after arrival at Alaska, by having sought to proceed to Fairbanks, or some place or other inland. The atmospheric conditions were here considerably better than they were at the same time along the coast. We should, however, in order to reach a place, have been obliged to fly over a thick belt of fog, which lay on the mountains in North Alaska, and this would have been a very risky enterprise. In flying over thick fog where drift-calculations are quite impossible one may little by little come far away from the place where one supposes oneself to be. If the flight proceeds in a mountainous region, when the altitude of flight is low, as is always the case with an airship, one then risks flying straight against a mountain-top which one imagined far away. The author is therefore of the opinion that the flight to Teller and the landing there was the most advantageous one that, under existing weather-conditions, could take place.

The account of the weather and of our work in

connection with the weather during the polar flight is herewith terminated, but we shall below add a few words regarding the scientific result of the flight.

It is perhaps a little bold to write about the scientific result of the polar flight whilst a part of the observations are still not worked out. However, we can already to a certain extent judge what will give results of somewhat great scientific value. Without a doubt the greatest result of the flight consists in the expedition having firmly proved that between the Pole and Point Barrow there does not exist any land, thereby finally settling an old scientific point of dispute.

There are several theories that maintain the existence of a fairly large continent on the stretch we flew over. Of these theories the one best grounded is that of the American, Mr. Harris, who, on the basis of tidal wave observations, believed he could prove the existence of a large piece of land north of Wrangel Island (Wrangelöen) and Point Barrow. Harris, amongst other things, thought that he could prove that the tidal wave which appears in East Siberia and on the north coast of Alaska moves from west to east, and this he thought argued the existence of a rather large continent north of these coasts. The results of his tidal-wave investigation are, however, in conflict with those of Dr. H. M. Sverdrup. On the basis of far better material, collected during the *Maud* expedition of 1922-5, he succeeded indeed in showing that the tidal wave comes in toward the coasts mentioned straight from the north, after having gone the whole way from Europe over a 3,000-4,000 meter deep Polar Sea. According to this, Sverdrup denies the existence of any particularly great land on the region crossed by the *Norge,* and the polar expedition has now confirmed his assertion.

The above result may well be regarded as purely geographical, but meteorological science should also have reaped a good deal of benefit from the polar flight. One of the problems that the expedition has brought to life refers to the polar fog. Why is it that over the monotonous plain which is formed by the Polar Sea there occur regions, close to one another, *with* and *without* fog, often without any changes in atmospheric temperature being observable? Are the lowermost air-layers so conservative that they can still, in the Polar Sea, retain memories from their more southerly existence? Or is the phenomenon due—which, however, appears incredible—to the variations in the heat development between the air and the underlying ice?

Good results may be expected from the atmospheric-electric observations on board, which were for measuring the contents of the air of positive and negative ions. These measurements will become of peculiar interest for this reason—that the supply of ions from below are shut off, which is not the case over any other fairly large region in the world. The instrument that was used in the measurements was placed at the disposal of the expedition by Dr. Behounek, of the Radium Institute in Prague, who is also going to work out the results with the meteorologist of the expedition.

Finally, the expedition gained some results which might be well called practical-meteorological. It proved that it is absolutely possible to fly over the Polar Sea with an airship even if the meteorological conditions should be quite unfavorable, as was the case during the later part of our voyage. On the other hand, we had so many difficulties when we were about to start, during the formation of ice-coatings and during the storm in Kotzebue Sound, that the writer has come to the definite conclusion that the airship traffic of the future over the Polar Sea—and some time there will be this traffic over this sea—is going to be carried on by aeroplane, with, let us say, eight motors, but one that can fly with four motors. Such an aeroplane ought to be the ideal one for polar flight. It is cheaper than an airship, not only in the purchase but also in the working, amongst other things because it does not require the assistance of a large party of men at the start and landing. It is swifter and more capable of resistance against storm and bad weather, and with its small surface, it does not run any particularly great risk of being weighed down to the ground by the formation of ice upon it.

B. L. GOTTWALDT

*The Norge's Radio Station and the
Radio Service on Board*

CHAPTER XII

THE "NORGE'S" RADIO STATION AND THE RADIO
SERVICE ON BOARD

FROM APRIL IOTH TO I4TH, 1926

On the 13th of November last year (1925) I was
suddenly called to the telephone. It was First-
Lieutenant Riiser-Larsen, speaking from Berlin,
who asked me if I would undertake to arrange for
the necessary radio-equipment to be procured for
the *Norge,* and at the same time he added that I
must myself go with them on the expedition. There
was nothing for it, of course, but to immediately
give a ready acceptance, both because it excellently
suited my newly started business as radio consult-
ing engineer, and not least, because a rapid trip to
the Pole does not fall to one's lot every day. I at
once set to work to find out what the various leading radio-firms could offer us in the way of radio-
equipment, and out of a number of tenders the Marconi Company was accepted as the most suitable for
our purpose.

In laying our plans for the apparatus-equipment
we took it for granted that the transmitter ought to
be made so powerful that it could, under ordinary
atmospheric conditions, maintain connection with

general coast radio-stations up to about 1,500 kilometers in the daylight, with an appropriate value-transmitter that had a wave length of between 600 and 1,500 meters. As the distance between Nome radio in Alaska and Svalbard radio in Green Harbour is something over 4,000 kilometers, we should then, if everything proceeded according to program, have only a stretch of about 1,000 kilometers on the other side of the Pole, from where connection with the outer world was doubtful. This supposition later proved to be estimated far too low, and if all things had gone normally we should certainly have been in direct radio-connection with the outer world during the whole tour.

The receiving apparatus must have great sensitivity and extend over a wave-length from 300 to about 25,000 meters, in order to be able to receive, in addition to the ordinary ship-range and coastal-station traffic, the time signals and the meteorological reports also that were sent out from various main stations in the world several times in the twenty-four hours.

During the flight from Svalbard to Alaska the large Trans-Atlantic Station, Stavanger radio (LCM) was obligingly placed gratuitously at the disposal of the expedition by the Norwegian Telegraph authorities; and this large station sent, in the course of the twenty-four hours, a number of important meteorological reports collected from the

The "Norge's" Radio Station

various European and North American weather-
forecasts. Moreover, twice in the course of the
twenty-four hours, Stavanger also sent out a time-
signal especially agreed upon, namely 7 A.M., that
is 6 A.M. Greenwich Mean Time (G.M.T.) and 7
P.M. (18 G.M.T.). The time signals were sent out
as follows:

Time-signal from LCM twice in the twenty-four
hours during the *Norge's* polar flight, 1926. All
times are reckoned by G.M.T. which is one hour less
than Norwegian normal time.

		H M S		H M S		
In the morning :	from	5 58 00	to	5 58 20	sent	v. v. v. v.
	"	5 58 20	"	5 58 40	"	LCM—LCM LCM—LCM
	"	5 58 40	"	5 59 00	"	v. v. v. v. v.
	"	5 59 00	"	5 59 55	"	second's beat
	"	5 59 55	"	6 00 00		Interval.
	"	6 00 00	"	6 00 03		sent in long dash the beginning of which thus gives the exact time.
	"	6 03 00		and onwards		for safety's sake were then sent the date and the month spelt out.
In the afternoon:	from	17 58 00	"	18 03 00		and onwards in the same manner as above with the date given at the close.

Accuracy with sending by hand about - 0.5.

All the meteorological reports were first collected
in Oslo, and, at hours arranged beforehand, sent out

from the Telegraph Department Central Office in Oslo over a land-line about 350 kilometers long, direct to Stavanger radio transmission apparatus.

During the flight telegrams and other announcements of interest were occasionally sent over this station, and not a single telegram appears to have been lost during the trip. Stavanger was invaluable to the expedition, and this large station worked admirably the whole time. We could thus without difficulty read Stavanger radio right down to Alaska even on direction-finder on board. Besides the ordinary transmitter and receiver equipment, the airship was also fitted with a special radio direction-finder on the Marconi system, with two large fixed frames and a radiogoniometer. The radiogoniometer was constructed for a wave-range from about 600 meters to 18,000 meters, so that one could take radio-bearings not only to ship and coastal stations, but also to the large Trans-Atlantic radio-stations, should it prove desirable. During the whole trip this wireless-bearing arrangement was of exceptional use for the navigation of the airship, as the bearings always proved quite correct and could be taken at a very great distance. Even accuracy of the bearing-apparatus was within about one degree; but it was not, of course, always so easy to get the bearings effected with certainty and accuracy because of the sharp and unexpected movements of the airship and the slowness of the ship's compass.

The "Norge's" Radio Station

This was especially noticeable during the uneven wind-conditions, of which we often had more than enough.

The electric generator of the station, which delivered both high and low tension energy, was driven by a small air-propeller which was mounted outside on an arm on the starboard side of the gondola. With the help of a cogged-wheel gearing and a coupling-shaft the power was then conducted to the generator, which was installed on a table at the after-part of the radio cabinet. With the help of a handle fixed inside the gondola, the boss of the air-propeller could be turned in such a way that the wind operated more or less on the propeller-blades, and in this manner the speed of the generator could be varied or entirely stopped.

In the event of a forced landing we had for the driving of the generator a two-cylinder air-cooled "Douglas" petrol motor of 3 h.p. that could be coupled with the electric dynamo on a separate, lightly-built base. For elevating the emergency aerial (which consisted of 150 meters of thin aluminium cable) we had with us a specially constructed box-kite which, with about a 5 meters wind, was capable of lifting a weight of from 3 to 4 kilograms.

We also had on board a two-valve short-wave receiver of Marconi's latest type for a wave-range of 10 to 100 meters. The object of this receiver was to try to get into communication with the short-wave station (KDZ) erected at Point Barrow by the *New York Times*. It worked quite well and was, for instance, used with excellent results on a little aerial at King's Bay during Commander Byrd's fine flight to the North Pole on the 9th of May. It was possible for us to follow him, almost continuously, on the whole of his 15½ hours' flight there and back. Just after our departure from King's Bay this receiving apparatus unfortunately fell on the floor when the airship made a very steep ascent, and was partially destroyed. Owing to lack of space we had indeed only fixed up the things loosely, and unfortunately we did not succeed in getting any more practice with the apparatus on the last part of our flight.

Before proceeding to describe the radio-service during the flight itself, it may perhaps be timely to give a short technical description of the various parts of the radio station. Such a brief analysis will go far toward explaining the installation and the various instruments. The radio-cabinet, which was about 2 meters long, 1 meter wide, and 2 meters high, was built in the after-part of the pilot-gondola on the starboard side. The cabinet was, in the after-part on the port side, furnished with a door, and in the ship's side to starboard there were placed two large celluloid portholes.

In the fore part of the cabinet a telegraph table

was fixed, and the transmitter was mounted on a teak board on the front wall. On the shelves on the port side the various receiving and tuning apparatus were placed, besides the radiogoniometer with its appurtenances. The aerial with its appurtenances, variometer and reaction-coil, stood on the floor under the table, just by the left foot of the wireless operator. Just behind was the leading-in insulator for the aerial mounted on the floor. On the starboard side on the wall the charging board was mounted and in the corners stood the high-tension batteries and accumulator-batteries. A small light folding chair served as support for the radio-operator. It was not more than just possible for one to get oneself, when in polar dress, in it. It took some time before one got accustomed to a position which gave least opportunity to elbows and knees for high-tension and high-frequency sparking from the various oscillating circuits. Just astern of and outside the cabinet stood the station's generator on the top of a slender wooden cupboard. This was then connected with the air-propeller through a coupling-shaft and a cog-wheel gearing. The four-bladed air-screw was constructed of hard wood, and gave about 3 h.p. at 1,800 revolutions. At full-speed the generator gave about 400 watts high-tension energy at 14 volts. The valve-transmitter itself was coupled direct to the aerial by the well-known Hartly-coupling, with parallel feeding of the lamps. The oscillations were produced by two 250 watts transmitter-valves arranged parallel. The telegraph key was placed in the grid-leak circuit and the transmitter could operate with continuous-wave signals (C. W.) or with tonic train signals (I. C. W.). For this purpose was attached a small motor-driven interrupter in series with the telegraph key. The aerial toning inductance consisted of a large cylindrical coil of thick, bare copper-wire with fixed tappings for the anode and the aerial coupling. For the aerial was used a single-wire phospher-bronze cable, 100 meters long and about 2 millimeters in diameter, which on the underside was furnished with a lead weight. For the purpose of speedy heaving-in of the air-wire there was a special winch with brake arrangement. The oscillation energy delivered to the aerial was by full charge a good 200 watts; the filaments of the transmitter-valves received their current from a small accumulator battery of 12 volts, which was kept continuously charged from the generator. The transmitter was tuned at 600, 900, and 1,400 meters, and was sometimes used at 900 meters, but mostly at 1,400 meters.

At 1,400 meters one had, with full charge of $5\frac{3}{4}$ amp. in the aerial, at 900 meters about $6\frac{1}{4}$ amp., and at 600 meters about $6\frac{3}{4}$ amp. by continuous wave transmission.

The "Norge's" Radio Station

In order to be uninterrupted as much as possible by the ordinary ship-traffic and for the correspondence at 900 meters for aircraft traffic, we nearly always used the 1,400 meter wave, which constantly gave very satisfactory results, both with regard to range and to durable work.

The receiving-outfit consisted of a special tuner with interchangeable coils. To this tuner was coupled a standard seven-valved detector with note-filter belonging to it and double low-frequency magnifier—in all eleven lamps. In addition there was a separate local oscillator for the reception of signals from stations that operated with continuous oscillations. All these valve-circuits mentioned here (with the exception of the tuner itself) could be coupled over to the radiogoniometer and be used in taking radio-bearings. The external frames of the direction-finder each consisted of two turns of well-insulated cable, which were placed round the balloon surface of the airship, right over the pilot-gondola: the frames were arranged at an angle of 45° with the ship's longitudinal axis, and both frames mutually formed an angle of 90°. The surface contents of each turn was about 400 square meters, so that the detection efficiency and accuracy of the radio-compass were in this way very great. As counter-weight both for the transmitter as well as for the receiver, the metal hull of the airship was used. All metal constructions, wires, gas-valves, etc., were carefully joined together with copper conductors, so that there were no detached parts which might possibly give occasion to dangerous sparking.

That everything acted satisfactorily is proved best by the fact that many times we inadvertently transmitted at full strength at the same time that the gas valves on the top of the airship were opened and still nothing happened; this should not, of course, be the usual practice in the future.

The radio material, constructed at the Marconi factories in England, was installed in Rome, but owing to some minor faults in the apparatus we had no opportunity of testing the various parts and instruments in the air before starting. The receiving apparatus and the radio-compass were, however, fully tested before we sailed, so that we could take it for granted that these parts would work correctly.

Before our departure from Ciampino, just outside Rome, extensive arrangements regarding the radio-service were made with the Italian, French, and English meteorological and military radio stations. It may perhaps be of interest to see how the meteorological service, etc., was arranged with the British Air Ministry. The well-known air-pilot and constructor, Major Scott, who accompanied the *Norge* from Rome to Pulham, had arranged the following service for the first stage of the tour.

The "Norge's" Radio Station

1. In the event of the airship proceeding from Rome to Pulham direct, the Basle Station call sign HB3 will relay traffic between Ciampino, Rome, and Air Ministry GFA, London.

2. Should the airship, however, proceed via Marseilles, arrangements with the French authorities will be made at Marseilles by Major Scott as to the route over which traffic shall be passed to the Air Ministry.

3. Major Scott will arrange for the wireless station situated at or near Ciampino to get into communication on 1,400 meters W/T with Basle at about midday on the 1st of April, at which time a routine will be drawn up between the two stations as to the disposal of traffic.

4. With reference to paragraph 7 of the attached Meteorological Memorandum for the Meteorological Office, the meteorological interception station will be re-opened at Pulham upon the receipt of instructions from the Superintendent, Airship Meteorology Division. The messages, according to the timetable shown in Appendix I, will be intercepted.

5. Arrangements will be made for notifications of the local occurrence of snow, thunderstorms, or

squalls to be sent direct to Pulham on 900 meters W/T or R/T from Cramwell and Sealand.

6. Occasional meteorological messages issued by the Meteorological Office (6) concerning this flight will be forwarded to the Meteorological Officer, Pulham, via Croydon; the procedure being that the message will be sent to Air Ministry Wireless Station, passed by direct telephone-line to the Duty Office, Croydon, and from Croydon to Pulham by 900 meters R/T (paragraphs 10 and 11 of Meteorological Memorandum).

7. In connection with paragraph 13 these messages will be handed in to the Air Ministry W/T Station by Meteorological Office (12) and will be passed to Basle for disposal to Rome, or alternatively through the medium of Le Bourget to Marseilles.

8. In connection with paragraph 16, this routine will be carried out on 1,400 meters W/T by the Air Ministry GFA direct. In connection with paragraph 17, this routine will be carried out on 900 meters W/T or R/T (depending on whether the ship is at extreme ranges or near enough to conveniently work R/T) by the Pulham or Croydon Stations as directed by Croydon. The call signs of the Pulham and Croydon stations are Croydon and GED and Pulham and GEP respectively.

9. In connection with paragraph 20, communications between the ship and Pulham will be carried

out on 900 meters R/T independent of other aircraft; working, if possible, on reduced power. In connection with paragraph 22, this routine will be carried out either on 1,400 meters W/T or 900 meters W/T or R/T dependent upon the position of the ship at the time concerned.

10. Immediately the ship passes the 200 miles radius of Pulham she will be treated as aircraft in flight within the British Control area, and as such will have available at all times for requirements the R/T and D. F. stations situated at Croydon, Lympne and Pulham.

Shortly after the airship had left the flying ground, Ciampino, at 9 A.M. on the 10th of April, we called up GFA, the Air Ministry, London, 1,400 meters, and our signals were at once taken up by this station. The distance was about 1,400 kilometers, which promised well for the range of our transmitter. Owing to great jamming from the adjacent Italian radio stations, several of which worked with about the same wave-length, it was, however, difficult to maintain any direct communication with England. The Air Ministry, however, followed our correspondence with Italian and French stations the whole time, and often took our signals direct, even if they were sent over stations lying nearer at hand. During the voyage over France, on the night between the 10th and 11th of April, we were mostly in communication with

First Crossing of the Polar Sea

Toulouse, Rochefort, and Le Bourget, near Paris. Owing to some bad plug-connections in the generator we had to cease the transmission for one and a half hours, but the machine was temporarily repaired and functioned satisfactorily. On the voyage to Pulham radio-bearings were often taken in order to see how everything worked, and even then these apparatus proved to be in full working order in spite of the fact that we had poor opportunity of correcting the direction-finder before departure.

On the voyage from Pulham to Oslo on the 14th of April, we got good use for the direction-finder, as we met fog between the west coast of Jutland and up towards Arendal. There was also arranged a special program from the British Air Ministry for this part of the trip. The program reads as follows:

AIR MINISTRY METEOROLOGICAL OFFICE

Arrangements for exchange of Meteorological Information between Pulham and *Norge* during flight from Pulham to Oslo April 13th-14th, 1926.

1. The Meteorological Office at Pulham will remain open continuously until the *Norge* has landed at Oslo.
2. Communication with Pulham will be:

The "Norge's" Radio Station

> (*a*) direct on 900 m. until the airship has reached a point distant 200 miles from Pulham.
>
> (*b*) via the Air Ministry on 1,400 m. when ship is more than 200 miles from Pulham.
>
> *In this case the messages should be addressed "Air Ministry repeat Pulham."*

3. The airship will notify Pulham (direct or via Air Ministry as the case may be) of her
> position
> altitude
> average air speed since last position
every two hours.

4. The Meteorological Office, Pulham, will stand by throughout to give meteorological information on request.
> In addition, a forecast will be passed to the airship, based on the 0100 chart of the 14th.

5. The Air Ministry will be notified from Oslo immediately the airship has landed there, so that the staff standing by at Pulham may go off duty.

The necessary meteorological announcements were always received without difficulty, and we had not flown far over the North Sea before we got into communication with the Norwegian coast-stations Flekkerö and Tjömö and later direct with Oslo radio on Tryvannshöiden.

The Norwegian telegraph authorities, at our request, most willingly permitted their coast-stations to listen specially for the *Norge* on 1,400 meters wave-length, and it was always only a matter of a moment to get into communication with them.

The voyage to Gatchina, slightly south of Leningrad, was made on the 15th of April without any complications worth mentioning. We kept connection the whole way with Swedish, Finnish, and Esthonian stations. It was rather more difficult to get hold of the Russian stations, but during the afternoon of the 15th of April we at last got the radio station in Kronstadt. In the thick fog over Sweden and the Baltic the direction-finder was constantly used, and proved, as usual, entirely correct and easy to manage.

On the 5th of May we at last left Gatchina and steered north-east over the great lakes Ladoga and Onega, towards the Murman coasts and Vadsö. This time we had no great difficulties in communicating with the Russian stations, as previously we had had the opportunity of conferring with the respective Soviet authorities as to wave-lengths, listening times, and the telegraph service. We signaled, took meteorological reports and bearings the whole flight northwards, and it may be mentioned that small vessels that lay in Vadsö and in King's Bay, Svalbard, 1,000 and 2,000 kilometers distant respectively, were able to hear our signals just after our departure from Gatchina. Of the stations we were in contact with may be mentioned those of Leningrad, Petrosavodsk, Archangel, Murman, Tromsö and Vardö. Our transmitter thus worked excellently and did not disappoint us. During the unsettled weather that we had over the great lakes, Olonkin suffered a temporary absence of mind, and in pure keenness for his work he inadvertently took hold of the transmitter's high-tension terminal and thereupon collapsed on to the floor, which fortunately stood this unlooked-for extra strain. By good luck the generator was running at only 1,000 to 1,500 volts pressure, and therefore his "absence of mind" was not of long duration, but he still remembers the shock. With full tension, however (3,500 to 4,000 volts), Olonkin would doubtless have remembered the terminal screw a good deal longer.

From Vadsö to King's Bay, Svalbard, the station worked remarkably well. We were the whole time in safe communication with all the Norwegian wireless stations both in North Norway and at Svalbard and Björnöya (Bear Island). With the help of our radio-compass we steered safely through the fog-banks; and when, for instance, we passed Björnöya, it proved that we had a direct course straight to the wireless station there. When we were right above it we caught a glimpse of the station through the fog. In the snowstorm along the west coast of Svalbard the radio-compass was again of good use, and it certainly would not have been difficult to navigate in thick and foggy weather all the way to King's Bay. The most important meteorological forecasts for the route over the Arctic Ocean were received from Tromsö wireless station, and afforded us special service.

During our stay at King's Bay it unfortunately transpired that our friend Olonkin the telegraphist had contracted a slight affection of the ear, which made his further participation in the flight impossible. We then engaged telegraphist Storm-Johnsen, who was at the time doing service at the little King's Bay station for the last part of the expedition, and he did very good work on the trip over to Alaska, and later on at Teller.

On the 11th of May, at 8.55 A.M. G.M.T., the last part of the journey began—the part that had been regarded with anxiety and excitement. During the stay in King's Bay we managed to go carefully over all apparatus to the smallest detail, so we had every hope of keeping long contact with the home-country even if the sun were visible both day and night. After our departure we first kept in communication with the small private wireless station at King's

The "Norge's" Radio Station

Bay, and afterwards with the large, coastal station at Green Harbour.

In order to accurately keep on the meridian of King's Bay up to the pole, the course was constantly corrected with radio-bearings, taken to King's Bay and later to Svalbard wireless station, and we also took, when opportunity offered, long-distance bearings to Stavanger wireless station, Nauen, and the large American stations in the vicinity of New York. During the flight northwards and for a good distance past the North Pole there were sent out in quick succession interesting Press announcements to the Norwegian Aero Club, for the most part in a code arranged beforehand. There were likewise both received and sent telegrams of greeting, amongst others to His Majesty the King, the Norwegian Government, the Parliament, various Italian higher authorities, in addition to a number of telegrams of more private character. Our wireless correspondence was also the whole time followed by the naval guardship *Michael Sars,* which during this time lay on the Finmark coast, its maximum distance being about 2,500 kilometers. So as to hasten the forwarding of our telegrams over Svalbard both Röst and Vardöy radio stations listened for our signals, and telegrams were taken by these stations until we were well past the Pole: that is to say, a distance of 2,300 to 2,500 kilometers.

First Crossing of the Polar Sea

From our good, faithful friend the far-away Stavanger wireless station we received, in addition to meteorological announcements and time-signals, the latest news and some private telegrams also. From the time of our departure from King's Bay until we lost wireless touch 55 radio telegrams (aggregating 1,583 words—i.e., 1,489 words transmitted and 94 received) were exchanged between the *Norge* and Svalbard. In addition to this should be added, "Service notes" and such-like. Particularly brisk was the traffic when the polar point was passed, and everything that could be thought of, such as flags and souvenirs, were thrown out over "the top of the world." All these details should indeed be solemnly reported to those who waited longingly in many lands. We had safe connection with King's Bay until midnight of the 11th May, and the distance was then about 1,300 kilometers. Later we kept to the powerful Svalbard station, which we communicated with for the last time at 7.30 A.M. G.M.T., on the 12th May. We were then about 500 kilometers over on the other side of the Pole, and the total distance was close on 1,900 kilometers. Our radio signals were still strong in Svalbard, and gave a signal-strength of R.7-R.8 (the maximum is R.10) whilst Svalbard's radio signals were still very powerful on board. They were, however, completely spoilt by the violent noise in the receiving apparatus which for the last few hours

THE WONDERFUL HAND SLEDGE MADE BY WISTING—OUR ONLY MEANS OF EMERGENCY TRANSPORT.

IN THE RIGGING DURING THE FLIGHT.

CONDITIONS OF THE POLAR ICE AS SEEN FROM THE "NORGE."

1. Vicinity of the Pole.
2. A great lead from an altitude of 1,500 feet.
3. Fringe of the Polar Pack.

"THE FASCINATION OF THE UNKNOWN."

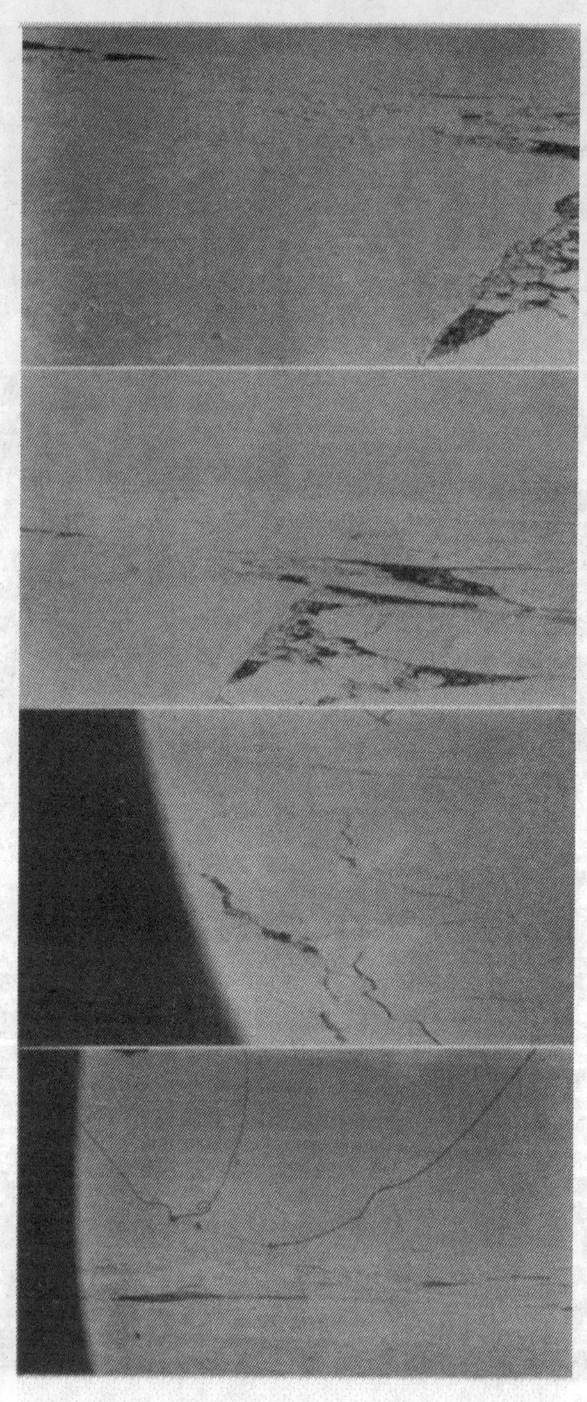

THE FIRST HUMAN VISION OF THE "GREAT UNKNOWN" LYING BETWEEN THE NORTH POLE AND ALASKA.

had arisen on account of the uneven motion of the air-screw. This in turn caused vibration in the generator, which had to be kept going during the reception, as the capacity of the batteries had gone down in the low temperature.

In order to obtain an impression how the radio telegraph service turned out on the voyage northwards and past the Pole, we will here include a report from the excellent Th. Mörk, wireless manager, King's Bay. In his own words the report is as follows:

Report of the telegraph service at King's Bay radio, from the airship *Norge's* departure from King's Bay at 10 A.M. on 11th May, 1926, until the ship was announced to have passed Point Barrow. (All times are calculated according to mid-European time.)

"At 9.50 on 11th of May, 1926, I have 'got the line' of the ever-obliging LFG (Svalbard), and let the motor run whilst, from the station-roof, I follow all the movements over at the hangar through my glasses. Ramm has just handed in his last telegram. It is to be sent off at the precise moment the *Norge* sails. It lies uppermost in the 'outgoing' pile. I wished to say something when he bade good-by, but got no opportunity for anything else than to clutch at him. In his haste he left his thermos-flask, so I have taken charge of it.

"At 10 o'clock the *Norge* casts loose. I wait a little until I hear the steady drone of the motor, and then rush in to send off the telegram of departure, whilst the airship slowly makes her way out of the fjord. I get acknowledgment 'O.K.,' and then listen-in on the *Norge's* wave-length. For a moment I hear nothing. With full power I send an earnest 'God protect the *Norge*,' and a moment later I hear Storm-Johnsen's 'Well, are you there?' Now comes the relief of the watch. Sandvei comes in smiling and tells me that he has taken some good photos of the start.

"The first telegram we send the *Norge* is a weather-forecast from Point Barrow to Roald Amundsen:

" 'Weather foggy. Barometer rising, light wind from East. Liebes.'

"When I came out I saw the *Norge* in the middle of the fjord off Cape Mitra. A splendid day. The *Norge,* with her crew, wrapped in ether waves, sails on into history.

"It is 23.00 o'clock the same day. Sandvei has had a busy time on watch: There are the reporters, then interruptions from the harbor, and finally connection with the *Norge,* which must not fail. He reports that the ship's transmitter is still to be heard strongly. Many telegrams are exchanged, just as the *Norge* has got our bearings and now steers north along our meridian.

The "Norge's" Radio Station

"It is now past midnight. We have sent a congratulatory telegram to Lincoln Ellsworth. To-day, the 12th of May, at the North Pole, he celebrates his 45th year.

"Sandvei still sits listening-in. Indeed, he has some difficulty in dragging himself away. He is as tough as Italian hemp. At 12.30 we get a telegram from Roald Amundsen, with the order 'From now onwards King's Bay Wireless Station will be exclusively at our disposal.'

"We feel freed from the reporter's yoke.

"I go on watch, and pass the night listening for the *Norge,* which chiefly corresponds over Green Harbour radio. Ramm's unique style of telegram is very attractive. The 'Harbour' disturbs me a good deal. Communication with the airship is certain until 8.34, then the *Norge,* after having sent out a Press-telegram, cannot hear either the Green Harbour or King's Bay station.

"At 8.42 the *Norge* calls: 'KDZ . . . give reply on 40 meters.' The airship repeats its call insistently, and at 8.45 we hear from Svalbard the light valve-transmitter LBT for the last time call: 'KDZ de LBT give reply on 40 meters.' She has given up listening for us.

"The distance between the airship and Svalbard station is probably 1,700 kilometers.

"The ship's 200 watts station is now heard here just as strongly as Vardö radio. I admire the airship's radio station. We have heard it strongly here, also during the voyage from Leningrad to Vadsö. We now without result listen for signals from LBT on interchangeable 1,400 and 900 meters wave-length until 16.15 o'clock, when we have orders from the representative of the Aero Club here, Lieutenant Höver, to renew the usual forwarding of telegrams, with listening duties, until further notice.

"We kept unbroken watch for twelve hours. After that there came a telegram from the Aero Club that the *Norge* had passed Point Barrow."

The following summary report from the manager of the Norwegian State's powerful wireless station at Green Harbour is also of much interest: Extract of watch-journal for Svalbard wireless station during the *Norge's* flight from King's Bay, and farther on over the Pole. (All times are in mid-European mean time.)

"*Norge* started from King's Bay on 11th May at 10 A.M. At 13.50 TUJ is in communication with LBT.

"Afternoon: Now at 20 o'clock LBT sends tfc here. Asks if he is strong, here LBT is m. qsa. Signal strength very nearly R-9. Night: 21.35 o'clock: LBT should report now, but hear nothing of him. Both LFG and TUJ call LBT in vain—

RFU calls LBT. 21.50 o'clock LEK communicates with LBT. LEK says qsu.

"Forenoon, 12th May: 0.40 o'clock: communication with LBT, who sends four messages here. R-8/R-9. 1.20 o'clock. TUJ has communication with LBT. From now onwards TUJ will cease all correspondence and listen only for LBT until to-morrow afternoon. 2.08 o'clock. Tfc from LBT. LBT says he will 'stretch himself a little' sl qsa. 3.30 o'clock. Tfc from LBT. R-8/R-9. 4.00 o'clock. Tfc from LBT OK. 4.30 o'clock (Px): 3.30 o'clock the NORTH POLE was passed. The motors were slowed down to 'slow' and the airship went down to low altitude. Then Amundsen first dropped the Norwegian flag, next Ellsworth the American Stars and Stripes, and finally Nobile the Italian flag on the polar ice. The flags were fastened to sharp poles, so that they remained standing, waving in the wind.

'LFG congratulates LBT and cheers, "Hurrah!"'

LBT's signal-strength does not seem to have become perceptibly less. Qsu 6.30: 6.30 o'clock LBT qsa R-8. Took seven telegrams to 6.55 as he shall have LCM. Says he comes back at 8 o'clock with two short ones, of which one is express. At 8.13

LBT sent a px. He announced two, but sent only one. Both LFG and TUJ called LBT, but he did not hear. 8.37 A.M. called LBT on LFG; do not hear answer yet. 8.42 send LBT v's and says KDZ, KDZ de LBT. Begs for answer on 40 meters. Signal-strength between R-7/R-8."

At 8 A.M. we endeavored to call up Point Barrow station, KDZ, but we could not get any answer on our short-wave receiver, which we had not repaired after the tumble immediately after the start from King's Bay the day before. The weather-reports and time-signals from Stavanger stations we could, on the contrary, read with ease in spite of all the rumbling in the receiver, and we had the latest weather-forecast quite complete at 9 P.M. ȯn the 12th of May. Even close to Point Barrow on the morning of the 13th the reception from Stavanger wireless station was strong. The weather forecasts obtained were of little value because they were considerably belated. On the morning of the 12th of May the airship entered a very troublesome ice-fog, which at once proved disturbing in various ways. Amongst others the aerial and the lead-weight were quickly covered with a hard, milk-white ice an inch thick, which made it quite impossible to transmit or receive signals. After a hard struggle we at last succeeded in hauling the aerial aboard and hacking the ice away, but as soon as the wire was again lowered the ice settled once more in a thick coating. So long as this ice-formation lasted it was out of the question to get messages transmitted, so we finally let the whole gear remain inside. The ice also formed on the air-screw of the generator, and this had the effect of greatly decreasing the speed of the motor, at the same time making it shake so violently that we expected the whole generator and transmitting gear to be jolted to pieces. Fortunately we at last emerged from this misery—but our receiving apparatus had then already received a serious crack which could never be satisfactorily repaired. The transmitting gear was, on the contrary, first-rate, and worked as before, that is, when circumstances were not too abnormal, as unfortunately often later occurred. On the night between the 12th and 13th of May, when we rapidly approached the north coast of Alaska, we repeatedly tried to call up Point Barrow, Nome, and Fairbanks wireless stations, the distance being about 1,200 kilometers. Neither we nor they heard anything. It was subsequently proved that our transmitter worked all right, as we got reports of our signals having been heard in the Bering Sea, as far as the Aleutian Islands, already before the North Pole was passed.

During the flight along the shore from Point Barrow and downwards to Bering Strait we again entered a troublesome ice-fog, and we twice lost our aerial, which simply snapped on account of the additional weight. We then put out one of the reserve aerials (of which we fortunately had three), but even this was not without risk, as we often were so close to earth that the lead bumped and leaped along the ground, which was as hard as stone. We feared that the lead would be slung up into the propeller and damage it, and therefore we had for the most part the aerial-wire hauled in during this part of the flight.

We repeatedly endeavored to get into communication with the various Alaska stations, Nome, Fairbanks, St. Paul, Cordova, and Yakutat, also with a couple of Russian stations on the Siberian coast, Anadyr and Scredne Kolymsk, but probably these stations suffered from the same atmospheric difficulties as we encountered. As often as was possible we broadcasted, however, that the *Norge* was in flight, and begged any possible receivers to have this announced to Nome or Fairbanks. We used both 600, 900 and 1,400 meter wave-lengths, both on the "undamped" and on the "tonic-train" signals. This broadcasting had been taken up at two or three places, but these stations were not able to reach Nome and Fairbanks. We succeeded, however, in keeping our radio-compass in order, as the frames were glued into the balloon cover itself, and in the afternoon we managed to hear a station that we imagined to be the longed-for Nome. This supposition subsequently proved to be correct, the distance from Nome then being about 500 kilometers. We took bearings at once, and now got (along with an astronomical position-line taken just before) an approximate idea of the airship's position. We did not let Nome slip from us any more, but took bearings from this station as often as possible, when it had communication with Fairbanks in Alaska. At the same time we tried to call up the station with the transmitter, but Nome remained silent, as usual. The only station in Alaska that had heard us was a little radio-station south of Nome, called Tacotna; it endeavored to get into touch with Nome, but this station did not respond. The main station, St. Paul, situated in the south part of Bering Sea, had also heard us several times, but it was impossible for us to get hold of this station with the radio-compass, owing to the very difficult weather conditions, which caused us to roll, pitch, and twist. We had our work cut out to hold fast to the unsuspecting Nome.

I have often wondered whether one of the reasons for the unfavorable transmission results over the very rugged country of north-west Alaska—in any case, on the shorter distances—might not possibly be caused by the lower part of the aerial being unpleasantly close to the earth's surface. Indeed, many times it acted as a veritable "sounding-machine." The radiation-phenomenon might then easily assume a reverse character, with the "top" down and "the earth" up. A part of the energy had presumably gone down into the ground, and the remainder had been sent up into the air, which, *summa summarum*, resulted in absolute ether chaos, which had no influence worth mentioning on the comparatively adjacent Nome wireless station.

On the 14th of May about 8 A.M., G.M.T., we landed at Teller, and the *Norge's* radio-station became a thing of the past.

We at once set to work getting an old ½ kw. ship's wireless set which we found there, and which had not been in use for several years. Sleep for the time being, therefore, was out of the question. After much work and trouble, coupling up and tuning, we at last got it into a fair working order. The aerial was made of four-stranded wire and was suspended between two wooden masts about sixty feet high. The earth connection was very poor, as the ground consisted chiefly of shingle and sand. The astonishment at Nome was certainly great when the people there at midday, local time, on the 14th of May, suddenly received a call from this insignificant station, which had not been heard for many years, and which before had seldom or never succeeded in covering the 125 kilometers that, over high mountains and deep valleys, lay between Teller and Nome. This small Teller station worked hard for just over a fortnight. Indeed, it worked far beyond its limits; and it was many thousand

The "Norge's" Radio Station

words that our small temporary station flashed out
into the world concerning the airship *Norge's* long
and exciting voyage over the everlasting desert of
ice, which hitherto it had not been vouchsafed to
mortal eye to behold.

Mr. Minister,

I am deeply conscious of the significance of this occasion. I am proud to be an American, prouder to-day than I have ever been in my life before, because I have been entrusted by my President to carry the flag of my country to the North Pole, to be left there together with those of Norway and Italy, in commemoration of the Transpolar Flight by the three nations who participated. Through the ages to come, Mr. Minister, may the significance of those three flags, lying entwined together in the bleak arctic waste, ever remain as a symbol between the nations who left them, because the spirit in which they were planted was one of devotion to a common ideal—"to seek—to find—and not to yield"—in an effort to add to man's knowledge concerning the planet on which he lives.

The significance of this occasion is deep with another meaning also which cannot be overlooked. We are upon the threshold of a new era in exploration—it is a milestone in the progress of civilization. For almost four hundred years the Arctic has zealously guarded her secrets against man's invasion. But man will ever persist until her last secret is won. What they may eventually be worth in dollars and cents no one can foretell, but the nations who have paid the price with their manhood to learn them will not have paid in vain, for there is a gain in "going exploring." The work in hand imperiously and ruthlessly demands many of the best gifts of manhood, both of body and of mind. It tempers the will for the conquests of difficulties, it is a school in manliness. But beyond that, driving man forward on the path of evolution, is its great illusion, its complete devotion to an idea. Out of man's passionate curiosity as to the ways of nature has come this civilization we live in. Man, peering into space, looking in every direction and striving to understand, is the creator and builder.

Lincoln Ellsworth.

10 April, 1926.

[319]

INDEX

A

Aalesund, 26
Abruzzi, Duke of, 127
Alaska, 102, 139, 146, 155, 193, 199, 204, 227, 238, 243, 248, 253, 257, 269, 275, 286, 288, 302
Alaska Steamship Company, 161
Alekto, 31 *et seq.*
Alesandrini (rigger), 86, 130, 244
Aleutian Islands, 159, 311
Algarson Expedition, 27
Ameland, 27
Amsterdam Island, 139, 201
Amundsen, Gustav, 57 *et seq.,* 243, 246
Amundsen, Roald, 13 *et seq.,* 59, 73, 74, 89, 113, 127, 131, 136, 142, 144, 145, 148, 193, 198, 199, 207, 211, 219, 224, 229, 242, 246 *et seq.,* 268, 306, 307, 309
Anadyr, 269, 312
Anderson (foreman), 32
Andrée, Solomon A., 273
Archangel, 301
Arctic Ocean, 263
Arduino (motor-mechanic), 130, 244
Arendal, 90, 298
Arild, Mr., 31 *et seq.,* 56
Atlantic Ocean, 269
Atlas, 41

B

Baltic Sea, 262
Basle, 295
Behounek, Dr., 282
Bellman, 245
Bellochi (rigger), 85, 111
Bennett, Floyd, 120
Berge (photographer), 118, 122
Bergen, 171-173, 258
Bergensfjord, 129, 162, 166, 167
Bergeron (meteorologist), 258
Bering Sea, 269, 311, 313
Bering Strait, 144, 146, 147, 221-223, 276, 311
Berlin, 285
Berta (housekeeper), 56, 123
Bjerknes, J., 258, 261
Björnöen Island, 27, 53, 106-107, 264, 269
Björnöya (Bear Island), 301

Bordeaux, 79
Bothnia, Gulf of, 93
Bourget, Le, 298
Brandal, Director, 25
British Air Ministry, 294
Brögger Glaciers, 30
Brooklyn, 166
Brun, Svend, 53
Bull, Ole Borneman, 167
Bundefjord, 15
Byrd, Richard E., 20, 48 *et seq.,* 104, 110, 117 *et seq.,* 135, 166, 266, 290

C

Caen, 87
Canada, 180, 204, 266, 269
"Cape Fly-away," 211
Capri, 69
Caratti (motor-mechanic), 130, 243
Cecioni (chief-mechanic), 130, 228, 244
Chantier, 48 *et seq.,* 104, 110, 122
Christiansand, 174
Ciampino, 64, 67, 69, 75, 86, 234, 294, 295, 297
Continental Express, 165
Coolidge, President, 317
Cordova, 269, 270, 312
Cramwell, 296
Croydon, 296 *et seq.*
Cuers, 29
Cygnus, 39

D

Dana, Mt., 28
Davies, Captain, 160
Denmark, 90
Dietrichsen, Leif, 13 *et seq.,* 174, 234
Diomede Islands, 224
Dornier Wal Seaplanes, 13

E

Eagle, 269
Ekeberg Flats, 40
Ekeberg Road, 91
Ellsworth, Lincoln, 13 *et seq.,* 73, 74, 123, 127, 132, 138, 193, 208, 246, 307, 309, 319
English Channel, 87
English Meteorological Institute, 261

Index

9 780898 752878